"No one can weave together the major characters and stories of the Bible with the daily struggles we all face like my dear friend Sammy Rodriguez. *Your Mess, God's Miracle* is a must read for every believer for the hour we are in."

Jentezen Franklin, senior pastor, Free Chapel;
New York Times bestselling author

"Spiritual vision is essential in the darkness of the world around us. *Your Mess, God's Miracle* invites us to live in the light and experience both sight and insight as Samuel Rodriguez opens our eyes to the reality of seeing the unseen and what matters most. I love this book and its theme!"

Dr. Jack Graham, senior pastor, Prestonwood Baptist Church

"When do we experience God at work in our lives? When everything's going well? When we're happy and healthy? My friend Sammy Rodriguez wisely points out that Jesus accomplishes His best work in the midst of our struggle—we just need eyes to see it. Let *Your Mess, God's Miracle* guide you and give you the perspective you need to allow God to turn your mess into a message!"

Greg Laurie, senior pastor, Harvest Christian Fellowship

"If you find yourself struggling in life and having trouble with believing God for a way out of your crisis, this book, *Your Mess, God's Miracle*, will give you the tools to get out of the pit and on your way to victory!"

Cindy Jacobs, cofounder and president, Generals International

"If you've ever felt disqualified from doing great things for God, Pastor Samuel's book *Your Mess, God's Miracle* will encourage and empower you. You'll discover that your greatest miracles germinate in 'messy' places, making them a crucial part of your journey toward your God-given destiny. I thoroughly recommend this book."

Russell Evans, senior pastor, Planetshakers Church

"Pastor Samuel Rodriguez is one of the significant prophetic voices of our generation. His new book, *Your Mess, God's Miracle*, is a must read. In this exciting volume, Pastor Sam takes the reader on a journey to help us see God's power at work in our present situation or mess. He uses accounts of blind people in the Bible to help open our eyes to God's miraculous promise. After reading *Your Mess, God's Miracle*, you will never see your situation the same again. I was blessed by this book, and you will be as well."

Dr. William M. Wilson, president, Oral Roberts University

"Wow! This fantastic book opens our eyes to who we are in Christ and what God is up to in all the mess, in us and in our world. Pastor Samuel, my dear friend, a voice to our generation, has unique insights for the Church that we need to listen to and 'see.' I know this message will help the prayer of Paul, 'the eyes of [our hearts] may be enlightened,' be fulfilled in you and me today."

Phil Pringle, senior pastor and founder, C3 Church Global

"Reverend Samuel Rodriguez is one of the most impactful Christian figures in modern history. Many leaders aim to influence their generation for good. Reverend Rodriguez has helped shape his own as the undisputed leader of the explosively growing Latino evangelical movement."

Reverend Johnnie Moore, author, *The New Book of Christian Martyrs*

"Pastor Sam has a unique way of articulating truth in a way that makes it accessible to readers of all levels of expertise, understanding and backgrounds. In *Your Mess, God's Miracle*, his passion to see all God's children thrive shines through. This book is a reminder that no matter where you are in your journey, you can expect a miracle."

Kevin Sorbo, actor, director, author

"In these turbulent times, Christians need spiritual sight more than ever. Using scriptural examples, personal testimonies and prophetic promises, Pastor Sam shows us how to see the unseen in order to discern God's work in our lives. Regardless of the challenges we face or the circumstances we are in, we will find spiritual strategies and principles to turn our mess into a miracle."

Pastor Luke Barnett, senior pastor, Dream City Church

"When the eyes of your heart are open, you will see the world and yourself from God's perspective. The Holy Spirit wants to encourage, enlighten and empower you with life-giving shifts. You are a culture changer. This book is theology on fire."

Jesse Bradley, senior pastor, Grace Community Church;
evangelist; creator of Reviving Hope

YOUR MESS,
GOD'S MIRACLE

YOUR MESS, GOD'S MIRACLE

The Process Is Temporary,
the Promise Is Permanent

SAMUEL RODRIGUEZ

Chosen
a division of Baker Publishing Group
Minneapolis, Minnesota

Published by Chosen Books
Minneapolis, Minnesota
www.chosenbooks.com

Chosen Books is a division of
Baker Publishing Group, Grand Rapids, Michigan

Printed in the United States of America

Library of Congress Cataloging-in-Publication Data
Names: Rodriguez, Samuel.
Title: Your mess, God's miracle : the process is temporary, the promise is permanent / Samuel
    Rodriguez.
Description: Minneapolis, Minnesota : Chosen Books, a division of Baker Publishing Group,
    [2023]
Identifiers: LCCN 2022036457 | ISBN 9780800762063 (cloth) | ISBN 9781493440832 (ebook)
Subjects: LCSH: Faith—Religious aspects—Christianity. | Conduct of life—Religious aspects—
    Christianity. | Hope—Religious aspects—Christianity | Christian life.
Classification: LCC BV4637 .R623 2023 | DDC 234/.23—dc23/eng/20220930
LC record available at https://lccn.loc.gov/2022036457

Cover design by Darren Welch Design

Baker Publishing Group publications use paper produced from sustainable forestry practices and
post-consumer waste whenever possible.

23   24   25   26   27   28   29   7   6   5   4   3   2   1

To Lauren, my tourniquet, my sunshine, Daddy's baby girl.

Go change the world!

Contents

Foreword

When Sammy Rodriguez and I began our friendship, I quickly learned that he is one of the most teachable leaders I have ever met. He is an accountable, humble man of God who strives to live a life of integrity. I know this because, years ago, Sammy asked me to be one of his mentors. I was honored and privileged that he asked me, and I was even more impressed by his desire to truly grow in his relationship with God. He wanted to be accountable as a husband, father, pastor and leader. To this day, he will say to me, "Now, don't forget, you can call my wife at any time and ask her how I'm doing."

Sammy and I have a great relationship and a tremendous friendship, and we make sure we connect as often as we can. There are many times we will be at an event together and see each other from across the room, and we will make a beeline toward one another to hug. Every time I see him, I feel like I'm with a brother.

It is easy to see that God has put a special touch on Sammy's life. When I think of my friend, I think of what the Bible says about John the Baptist—"a man sent from God" (John 1:6). It would be easy for a man like this to not remain humble and teachable, but as you read the pages of this thought-provoking book, you'll sense the voice of a man who leads with humility and has a strong knowledge of God's Word. It is remarkable to see just how much Scripture Sammy was able to put into this book along with incredibly practical ways to apply it. His objective is to help people to grow personally *and* in their relationship with the Lord, and to see a glimpse of the *permanent* work He is doing in their lives.

As someone who has led a church for more than two decades, I have seen so many people in my congregation become hopeless and stagnant when they find themselves in messy circumstances. One of the keys to helping people in these situations is to help them take their eyes off their problems and put them on Jesus. In this book, Sammy does an excellent job of inviting readers not to confuse the temporary journey with the ultimate destination.

There is such a need for people in the body of Christ to walk in faith and know that God has a plan and a purpose for their lives. If there is an area of your life you think you've messed up and can't be redeemed, I am here to tell you that you can't mess up too much for God! He has a greater plan for your life than you could ever imagine. In fact, the Bible is full of stories about God taking people out of their messes and restoring them, such as the blind man Jesus healed by spitting in the dirt and putting a muddy mixture on his eyes. As you read through the following pages, you will see Sammy return to this story time and time again. This is such an important, foundational story because there are many areas in our lives in which we have been blinded and find ourselves in a mess.

As you make your way through this book, I encourage you to ask the Holy Spirit to open your heart and eyes to see any area in need of help. Allow Him to begin working in your heart so you can experience a breakthrough. If you find yourself in a mess, whether it's one you made or a circumstance you can't control, I believe God wants to do a miracle in your life. I pray that as you read Sammy's words, you'll allow God to step into your mess and open your eyes.

Robert Morris

Senior pastor of Gateway Church, bestselling author
of *The Blessed Life, The God I Never Knew,*
Beyond Blessed and *Take the Day Off*

Sight Unseen

Open Your Eyes to Your Blindness

Our God is not only the God who restores.
Our God is a God who gives us what we have never had before!

Learning to see is a lifelong process.

Physically, your vision usually develops over the first two years of life if your eyes are healthy. Just as babies must learn to walk and talk, they learn to see as their eyes begin working in tandem to distinguish the world around them as their body grows and matures. For the first four months, infants are attracted by large shapes and bright colors but cannot usually discern depth and distance. Gradually, they begin following moving objects and people and reaching for them, which is the genesis of eye-hand coordination.

Around five months old, babies' eyes work in sync to produce three-dimensional perception of their surroundings. The rods and

15

cones in their eyes develop more fully so that colors look more vivid in a variety of hues and tones. As they approach their first birthday, many babies have transitioned from crawling to walking, aiding in their coordination and ability to judge distances within their field of vision. By their second birthday, little ones can see amazingly well, with eye-hand coordination and depth perception usually developed fully.[1]

But learning to see is more than just the physical development of our eyes, because there are many ways to see.

The Eyes of Your Heart

Intellectually, seeing is often used synonymously with observing, comprehending and processing the data your senses relay to your brain. People who "get it" see connections and reach conclusions, often filtering what their eyes see or read with their personal experiences and observations. This kind of perception enables them to solve complex problems and recognize the way puzzle pieces fit together, whether in a logical, linear fashion or a more associative, intuitive method.

When it comes to your emotions, seeing refers to empathy, compassion and your awareness of your own feelings and the feelings of others. In recent years, the phrase "emotional intelligence" has evolved from a leadership buzzword to a mainstream concept, referring to your ability, both innate and cultivated, to recognize the emotions of others and see issues and situations through their eyes. Emotional vision allows you to read body language and interpret what is left unsaid, translating what is written between the lines for greater clarity and comprehension of the communication between individuals and within groups.

Spiritually, seeing goes beyond our physical, intellectual and emotional senses and abilities and becomes a matter of faith, which matures over time as we learn to trust God for all we need and in all areas of our lives. Faith requires confidence in what usually cannot be seen by our human faculties. "Now faith is confidence in what we hope for and assurance about what we do not see" (Hebrews 11:1).

Addressing the followers of Jesus who came after His ascension into heaven, Peter wrote, "Though you have not seen him, you love him; and even though you do not see him now, you believe in him and are filled with an inexpressible and glorious joy, for you are receiving the end result of your faith, the salvation of your souls" (1 Peter 1:8–9). With a similar goal in mind, Paul encouraged the believers at Ephesus, "I pray that *the eyes of your heart* may be enlightened in order that you may know the hope to which he has called you" (Ephesians 1:18, emphasis added).

SOMETIMES YOU CAN READ THE EYE CHART PERFECTLY BUT REMAIN BLIND TO YOUR OWN HEART.

Spiritual vision clearly does not rely on the accuracy of our ocular organs, the eyes. Regardless of how well our pupils, irises and corneas work in harmony with our optic nerves, we can glimpse God's power, presence and purpose in our lives if we walk in faith by the power of the Holy Spirit. Conversely, a person's physical vision may be 20/20 while they remain blind to spiritual matters. No matter how healthy, wealthy and stealthy someone may be, their spiritual vision relies on their relationship with Jesus Christ.

Sometimes you cannot read the fine print, but you can see clearly what matters most. Sometimes you can read the eye chart perfectly but remain blind to your own heart.

Divine Dose of Double Vision

This doubly ironic condition of being blind and seeing compared to seeing but being blind is at the heart of one of Jesus' most profound and provocative miracles. In fact, the situation surrounding this miracle is as fascinating as the method Jesus employed to give sight to a blind man He encountered. This encounter illustrates the convergent collision of physical healing and spiritual blindness and explores the dilemma of human suffering from an eternal perspective. Notice the sequence of events:

> As he went along, he saw a man blind from birth. His disciples asked him, "Rabbi, who sinned, this man or his parents, that he was born blind?" "Neither this man nor his parents sinned," said Jesus, "but this happened so that the works of God might be displayed in him. As long as it is day, we must do the works of him who sent me. Night is coming, when no one can work. While I am in the world, I am the light of the world." After saying this, he spit on the ground, made some mud with the saliva, and put it on the man's eyes. "Go," he told him, "wash in the Pool of Siloam" (this word means "Sent"). So the man went and washed, and came home seeing.
>
> John 9:1–7

On one hand, the narrative is simple and straightforward. As Jesus and His disciples were out walking, they saw a man who had been blind from birth. The disciples asked their Master a question about the cause of the man's congenital condition, and Jesus likely surprised them with His answer. Then He spat on the ground, again probably not what anyone expected, made mud with His saliva and the dirt, then spread the mud over the blind man's eyes. Then Jesus told the man, with his eyes still covered in this mud mask, to wash himself in the nearby Pool of Siloam. The man went there, washed and returned *seeing*.

Considered from another perspective, we glimpse a paradigm for how God often chooses to meet us in the muck and mire of our greatest trials and produce a miracle of healing and wholeness. And I do not know about you, but even after reading and reflecting on it dozens of times, I still find this encounter intriguing. Because the blind man presented an opportunity not only for the miracle of healing but for addressing the origin of his condition. In addition to this divine dose of double vision, the way Jesus healed this man is unexpected to say the least.

First, Jesus spits on the ground, which was not any more customary or socially acceptable then than it is now. Simply put, it is messy. We do not often think about the Son of God, our Lord and Savior, performing an action that is probably considered uncouth by most social and cultural standards. I remember as a kid how my mother would react if she saw me sneeze without a tissue or, heaven forbid, spit out my bubble gum—let alone landing a nice wad of spittle on the sidewalk. Polite, well-behaved kids did not spit, at least not in public.

As if spitting was not enough to get the attention of the disciples and others who paused to watch, Jesus then used His spit to make a little puddle of mud. What was already messy became messier. Again, I do not know your habits, and after reading what Jesus did here, I would never judge you. But most adults do not spit and then reach down and use the salivary solution they just ejected to create mud. I mean, mud made the natural way—with dirt and rain—is bad enough, right? Most of us do not like stepping in mud puddles and getting our shoes dirty, but there was Jesus, deliberately mixing up a batch.

His peculiar behavior then went one step further: *Jesus put the mud on the blind man's eyes.* We are reaching maximum messy here, what most of us would regard as downright gross. If we saw one of our kids on the playground spit, make a little mud cake and then start to smear it over another kid's eyes, we would be rushing to stop them before you could say, "Time out!" But this was no toddler improvising brown fingerpaint. This was an adult man, the Messiah, the Son of God.

Messy to Miraculous

Or think about this incident from another point of view. Just consider how you might feel if you had been in the blind man's sandals. You have been blind since birth, so you have never witnessed the glorious reds and golds of a sunrise. You have never looked on the faces of your parents, family and friends. You have never glimpsed the vibrancy of a rainbow arching across a turquoise sky. You have never seen your reflection in a mirror or the food you put in your mouth. Darkness is all you know.

Then one day you are sitting by a busy corner, most likely begging because you are unable to work, when a group of strangers comes along. You hear them talking and discussing a question you have pondered many times. *Why me? Why was I born blind when most others can see?* The next thing you know, one of the strangers reaches down, touches something on the ground and then places it over your eyes. And that something feels gooey and earthy just like—mud?

Yes, there is little doubt that Jesus' unorthodox method piqued everyone's curiosity. And as the Son of God, He certainly did not have to heal the man this way—He could have healed the blind man instantly without saying a word. So the fact that Christ chose to do it this way must be significant—amplifying the message it delivers with a wellspring of hope for us today.

Regardless of what the blind man might have thought or felt in that moment as the cool paste of earth and divine saliva enveloped his closed eyes, there is no indication he hesitated when Jesus instructed him to go to the Pool of Siloam and wash himself. And his unwavering obedience was rewarded with the gift of sight—something he had not experienced until that moment.

> NO MATTER HOW MESSY THE METHOD, THE MASTER HAD MANAGED A MIRACLE.

Can you just imagine him there, splashing water from the pool, rinsing away the caked-on dirty mask dripping down his face? But as he kept splattering water onto his face, suddenly he could sense a change. Something was different. Fluttering his eyelids, he felt light pour into his pupils as blurry forms took shape—he could see! Not only could he see, but he could see perfectly, with the kind of clarity, colors and coherence that could only come from the living God. Yes, the technique used seemed a little crazy, but the results were undeniable.

No matter how messy the method, the Master had managed a miracle.

Blind Spots and Blindfolds

I pray that you have never experienced blindness. Nonetheless, most of us have endured times when we felt in the dark, unable to see where we were or how to proceed. Just as sight has many layers and metaphoric implications, blindness does as well. And sometimes the worst kind of blindness is the kind that escapes your awareness. If you want to experience deeper intimacy with God, a closer walk with your Savior and greater reliance on the Holy Spirit, then you must be willing to open your eyes to areas of blindness in your life.

We have all heard of blind spots and being blindsided, which reminds us that no matter how well we think we see and know what is going on in our lives, we can rarely see everything going on—at least, not naturally. Sometimes we may feel blindsided by circumstances so sudden and unexpected they leave us reeling in their wake. Having your job terminated when you had just been given an excellent review by your boss. Overhearing your best friend gossiping to others about a secret you shared in confidence. Learning of a spouse's betrayal when you felt the love between you was unshakable. Discovering your teenager's addiction to prescription medications stolen from your own medicine cabinet.

Other kinds of blindness often result from our unwillingness to see what is right in front of us. Whether out of fear, uncertainty, denial or an attempt to control our lives, we ignore the aches and early symptoms in our body, pretending nothing is wrong with us so we do not have to see our doctor to have it checked out. Afraid to confront our coworker about the budget shortage, we look the other way until someone accuses us of embezzling or misappropriating funds. Unwilling to talk through our painful feelings with our spouse, we let the silence grow until we barely know one another.

Even when you have invited Jesus into your life as Lord and Savior and welcomed the Holy Spirit to dwell in your heart, you may still experience times of blindness. These include moments when you refuse to recall the truth in order to justify giving in to temptation. Days when you tell yourself there are no consequences for the secrets you keep. Times when you cannot see how far you are drifting away from God when you stop going to church. When you hang out with people who encourage you to do things you know God does not want you to do. When you turn to old habits and addictions to numb the pain of life's storms. When you ignore consequences—at work, at home, at school or at church—until they cannot be ignored.

The encounter between Jesus and the blind man reminds us to examine our blind spots and to exercise our spiritual vision as much as possible. Blindness is a condition that you can experience when you take your eyes off Jesus. When succeeding at work eclipses your commitment to loving and serving your family the way you know God wants you to. When focusing on your status and popularity on social media consumes the time you once spent with Him in prayer. When pursuing money or obsessing over what you do not have overshadows gratitude for the many blessings God continues to pour into your life.

Anytime you lose sight of God, the devil tries to blindfold you and keep you from seeing the truth.

False Fabrics

One of the most effective fabrics used by the enemy to blind you is despair. If he can convince you—or set you up to convince yourself, as is often the case—that your circumstances are hopeless, then he knows your spiritual vision has been impaired. When you cannot see any way to get out of the abusive relationship, the enemy is blindfolding you. When you are ready to give up financially because you believe you can never get out of debt, that is the devil darkening your spiritual vision. When the doctors have exhausted known treatments and left you writhing in the agony of your body's condition, then Satan wants you to believe that your situation is hopeless. When you long to change careers but fear you could never take such a bold risk, the enemy enjoys keeping you stuck in place.

Another fabric the enemy uses to blind us to God's truth is shame and false guilt. If the devil can weave these two heavy burdens together into a dense shroud, then he knows you will eventually collapse under its weight. This is not the holy conviction of a healthy conscience arising from the Holy Spirit in you. No, the enemy wants you feeling guilt unnecessarily, even after you have asked for and received forgiveness from God and those you have offended. Satan wants to sideline you by not simply triggering feelings of guilt for what you have done, but by creating shame about who you are. Guilt relates to what you have done; shame goes to the core of your identity.

When blinded by shame and false guilt, you are susceptible to the devil's lies that obliterate your perception of truth. "You're so weak and needy that you will never remain clean and sober," the demons whisper. "You will never manage money well so why don't you quit trying? You're a loser who was born poor and you'll die poor. You can never get out of debt so you might as well buy what you can while you can."

And when the enemy starts attacking your worth, then the darkness seems thicker than ever. "You're pathetic—no one will ever love you. Not once they get to know who you really are. You've messed up too many times for her to forgive you again. Once he sees who you really are, you'll be rejected and abandoned."

The enemy of your soul will even try to use shame to blind you to the truth of how God sees you. "If God loves you so much, why won't He help you overcome this addiction? Why are you still struggling in your marriage? With your kids? In your job?" Once seeds of doubt are planted, they begin to take root and try to block your view of who God says you are. The devil tells you that you are a liar, a thief, a gossip, a cheater, a fornicator, an adulterer, a murderer or a hopeless mess that can never be loved or redeemed. But this is simply not true.

Old labels may have reflected some of your past behaviors, but they can never define you once you have experienced the grace of

God and the indwelling power of the Holy Spirit. The Bible makes it clear: "And such were some of you. But you were washed, you were sanctified, you were justified in the name of the Lord Jesus Christ and by the Spirit of our God" (1 Corinthians 6:11 ESV). Do not allow the devil's accusations to blind you to who you really are.

Because you are not who you used to be.

You are not where you were.

You are not how you used to be.

You are not what others did to you.

You are not what you did to yourself.

You are who God says you are.

You are what God says you are.

It is not about how others see you or how you see yourself—it is about who you are in Christ. When you know who you are in Christ, then you will never be blinded by old labels and the devil's lies. Your identity in Christ will bring an end to your blindness.

It is time—today is the day you wash away the mud of past mistakes and open your eyes to your glorious future. It is time to become *who you already are.* And who are you? You are God's masterpiece, His beloved child, a co-heir with His only Son, Jesus Christ. "For we are his workmanship, created in Christ Jesus for good works, which God prepared beforehand, that we should walk in them" (Ephesians 2:10 ESV).

The good news is that God wants you to see clearly. He is opening your eyes to His truth even amid the mess of where you are right now. What Jesus did for the blind man that day is what He will do for you—if you are willing to trust Him through the mess.

Opportunity for the Impossible

Surely the blind man, whose eyes had not functioned properly since birth, must have assumed there was no hope that he would see. It would be one thing if he had lost his vision from disease as a child or because of an injury as an adult. Then he would know what he was missing, which might spark just enough hope that he could see once again. But this was not the case. This man had never been able to see. Surely he did not expect to receive something he had never had in the first place.

And based on the questions the disciples asked Jesus—"Is it this man's fault that he's blind? Or is he being punished for the sins of his parents?"—the blind man probably carried a burden of shame for his condition. He had likely heard plenty of people, perhaps even family and friends, ask the same questions. Aware of his blindness since birth, this man must have felt at times that he was the victim of grave injustices. Why should he be punished for something his parents did? And what could he possibly have done as an infant to deserve such cruel punishment, the deprivation of his sight? Eventually, this man might have started believing that somehow his blindness was his fault.

But Jesus corrected such faulty thinking before He proceeded to give this man his sight: "'Neither this man nor his parents sinned,' said Jesus, 'but this happened so that the works of God might be displayed in him'" (John 9:3). The blind man's condition was not a punishment or even the consequence of anyone's sin. It was an opportunity for God's power, glory and goodness to be showcased. The answer Jesus gave to the disciples reframed the way they perceived the blind man's condition, and it continues to shift the paradigm of our perception today.

What if the suffering, pain and struggles you are facing are similar to the blind man's condition? What if they are not an injustice to endure but an opportunity to showcase God's glory? Have you ever considered that you are not being punished when you are faced with challenges, but rather you are being presented with the potential for experiencing the miraculous, omnipotent power of God? This has happened so that the works of God might be displayed in you.

And, my friend, no matter what you are facing—blindness, cancer, bankruptcy, divorce, addiction, homelessness or betrayal—nothing is impossible for God.

Throughout the pages of Scripture and across the centuries, this refrain continues to echo. No matter what you are going through, no matter how dire the circumstances, no matter how unbelievable your loss or unfathomable your pain, you are more than a conqueror through Christ Jesus! What you perceive as impossible is simply an incomplete vision obstructed by your human limitations. Jesus said, "With man this is impossible, but with God all things are possible" (Matthew 19:26). When you have the power of the Holy Spirit within you, then you can move mountains with faith as small as a mustard seed (see Matthew 17:20).

I am convinced that God is attracted to impossible circumstances.

Show Him a barren womb.

Show Him a closed door.

Show Him a broken heart.

Show Him a shattered dream.

Show Him a bad medical report.

Show Him an empty bank account.

Show Him a dysfunctional family.

Show Him your need, and get ready for God to show up!

We are promised, "For no word from God will ever fail" (Luke 1:37).

He gave Abraham a word, and it never failed.
He gave Moses a word, and it never failed.
He gave Joshua a word, and it never failed.
He gave Hannah a word, and it never failed.
He gave Elijah a word, and it never failed.

And God gave us not just *a* word but *the* Word: "In the beginning was the Word, and the Word was with God, and the Word was God. . . . The Word became flesh and made his dwelling among us" (John 1:1, 14). Our Abba Father God gave us Jesus, the Word, and He has never failed!

The Lord has a word for you now, so get ready for the impossible. Your family is about to give birth to something amazing that will have an impact on generations. In your family, get ready for the impossible to take place. In your faith, get ready for the impossible to take place. In your finances, get ready for the impossible to take place.

Open up your mouth, speak into your house and say, "The Word of God will never fail!" I dare you to look into your bank account and say, "The Word of God will never fail!" Speak into that relationship that is full of drama and proclaim, "The Word of God will never fail!" I dare you to text your children and declare, "The Word of God will never fail!" I do not care how impossible it looks today—God is about to show up!

He is attracted to the impossible so that no human can get credit for what He is about to do. Your God is the God of the impossible.

Miracle from a Mud Pie

I know God can do the impossible, you might be thinking, *but I'm not sure He's actually going to do the impossible in my life.* Perhaps you consider experiencing God's miracles like winning the lottery or inheriting a windfall from a distant relative. *These things happen, but what are the odds that they will happen to me? Not very likely,* you conclude. Better to rely on your own power, ambition and tenacity to achieve results, **YOUR GOD IS THE GOD OF THE IMPOSSIBLE!** you assume. That is surely better than some pie-in-the-sky miracle from a mud pie.

But that is the exquisite beauty illustrated by how Jesus healed the blind man. Of all the ways the Lord could have given this man his sight, Christ deliberately made a mess as the precursor to the miracle. Why? Could it be to remind us that nothing is impossible for God? That even the most unlikely, unexpected messes can become fertile soil for harvesting God's power?

If you are struggling with applying the blind man's encounter with Jesus to your own life, then allow me to share your discomfort. In fact, let me confess something that you probably will not find shocking if you know me: I have a bit of obsessive-compulsive disorder (OCD). I like order and organization, efficiency and productivity. Schedules, lists and agendas help my world run smoothly and on time. I like focusing on preparation, solutions and resolutions as quickly as possible in order to move on to the next challenge. My mind works in a very linear, sequential manner. For all the Trekkies, I may preach revelation like Captain Kirk, but I process information like Mr. Spock.

Accordingly, I find it a bit challenging to reconcile what I perceive as utter chaos with miraculous order. In other words, how can such a miracle emerge out of a mess? This is why this biblical narrative speaks to me—because I have lived it. I have been blind to temptations until it was too late, blind to the heartaches of others and blind to my own selfishness at times. I need the messy miracle that only Jesus can perform in order to see clearly. And not simply to see clearly, but to open my eyes to what I have never seen before.

Because that is what this incident is all about.

As Jesus was walking along, He saw a man who had been blind from birth. Notice that this man was not losing nor had ever lost his sight. He never had it in the first place; he was born blind. You see, this circumstance facilitates the environment for Christ to reveal a functional miracle, an ontological extension of the creative nature of Providence.

With the woman who had the issue of blood, Jesus gave her back her health (see Matthew 9:20–22). With the invalid man at Bethesda, He gave him back his walk (see John 5:1–15). With Lazarus, He gave him back his life (see John 11). With another blind man (see Mark 8), He gave him back his sight.

But with this blind man, Jesus did not give him something he lost. Jesus gave him something he never had in the first place. For, you see, there is a difference between God restoring something you had and God giving you something you never had in the first place.

Our God is not only the God who *restores*. Our God is a God who *gives us what we never had before*. Our God is Lord of doing what has not been done before. His Word tells us, "See, I am doing a new thing! Now it springs up; do you not perceive it?" (Isaiah 43:19). Some of us focus our time on getting back what we lost when we should be asking God to give us what we never had in the first place.

God is not interested in renovating your past. He is more interested in releasing your future. Are you ready to see what you have never seen before? To experience what you have never experienced before? To go where you have never gone before? Then get ready, because you are about to give birth to the impossible. Get ready to sing and shout for joy! "'Sing, barren woman, you who never bore a child; burst into song, shout for joy, you who were never in labor; because more are the children of the desolate woman than of her who has a husband,' says the LORD" (Isaiah 54:1).

God is giving you sight to see what you have never seen before. He is birthing a miracle in the midst of your mess. From the spit and mud of your life, get ready to discover His priceless gift. Remove the blindfold and take off your mask. Recognize the areas of blindness that are being transformed.

Open your eyes to what you have never seen before!

──── OPEN YOUR EYES ────

At the end of each chapter, you will find a few questions to help you reflect on the main points we covered and how they apply to your life. Do not feel burdened or think of it as homework. While you do not have to write down your responses, you might be surprised to discover how helpful it can be to keep a record of how God speaks to you as you read each chapter.

Whether you record your answers or not, after you have spent a few moments thinking through these questions, I encourage you to go to the Lord in prayer and share with Him what is going on in your heart. To help ignite your conversation with God, you will find a short prayer. No matter what you are facing, remember that He is your heavenly Father, your Creator and the Lover of your soul. *Open your eyes to the new thing He is doing in your life!*

1. What are some blind spots or areas of struggle in your life right now? What burdens are you carrying that impede your journey of faith? What has kept you going this far?

2. In what ways do you relate to the blind man in John 9? What has obstructed your view of God's truth in your life? What lies of the enemy have been blindfolding you?

3. How have you seen God at work in the midst of your life's muddy mess? What do you need from Him most right now?

Dear God, allow me to see You with the eyes of my heart. Remove the lies of the enemy that are blinding me to Your truth, and cleanse my vision of old labels that impede my view. Thank You, Lord, for the new thing You are doing in my life, the miracle You are bringing to life. Give me courage to slog through the mud and to endure the mess because I know You are birthing a miracle in the messiness. May Your Spirit empower me so that I can know Your strength, stamina and security as I learn to see with new eyes. In Jesus' name, Amen.

Bless Your Mess

Open Your Eyes to the Power of Jesus

Your mess is the soil for God's miracle.

When Christ restores your vision, you will see His power unleashed in your life.

If beauty is in the eyes of the beholder, then messy is often just as subjective.

I will never forget the dilemma a good friend faced with his aging mother. He had been asking me to pray for her without specifically describing the root of the problem. The most he would disclose was that she struggled with her mental health. Then one afternoon, I got to see not only the evidence of this woman's issues, but the environment that had shaped my friend as a child.

He and I met for lunch at one of our favorite restaurants. Near the end of our meal, his phone rang. I could tell by the pained look on his face that he felt torn about answering it.

"Go ahead, my friend," I assured him. He nodded his appreciation, answered the call and began speaking rapid-fire Spanish that
even I had a hard time keeping up with. The caller was apparently
a family member who was requiring my friend's urgent assistance.

As it turned out, the caller was his mother. She could not find
her glasses and desperately needed them to read the prescription
labels on her medications in order to take the correct dosage. My
friend had picked me up from my office and insisted on dropping
me off before heading to his mom's.

"But doesn't she live just a few blocks from here? I'm happy to
go with you. It always helps me to meet someone I'm praying for."

"No, that's okay, Pastor Sam," he said, clearly distressed. "I don't
mind driving you back first. Besides, I'm not sure I want you to
meet my mother."

"Come on," I said. "It will only take a few minutes. I can even
wait in the car if you prefer."

Despite his reluctance, he drove the few blocks and pulled up in
front of a small brick ranch-style house in a family-friendly neigh-
borhood of similar homes. The yard could have used some attention, but with the drought we had been experiencing in California,
so could my own.

"You can come with me," he said, "because I will probably need
your help to find her glasses."

"Happy to," I said. "Lead the way."

We got out of his car and walked to the front door. "I need to
warn you before we go in," he said, with his hand on the doorknob.
"But there's no way I can prepare you for what you're about to see."

I shrugged and smiled, nodding for him to proceed. "Remember,
I'm a pastor. I've seen just about everything. It will be okay."

But my friend was right. Nothing could have prepared me for
what was behind that door. Actually, even opening the door proved

to be a challenge because of the assortment of cardboard boxes, garbage bags and stacks of magazines piled in the entryway.

Pushing aside the assortment to clear a path for us, my friend stepped forward and called out, "*Mamita*? I'm here—I have my friend Sam with me."

As we made our way down a narrow path, I marveled at the way every nook, cranny and surface featured overflowing collections of glassware, porcelain figures, Mexican pottery, seashells, wooden carvings and colorful vases. More stacks of boxes, magazines and books came up to eye level. Rather than someone's home, the place resembled a thrift store that had swallowed a houseful of furniture, or a storage unit that was prepared for a flea market.

Making our way into what must have been the kitchen, I saw piles of electronic devices and small appliances heaped like an art installation. Dozens of paintings, pictures and framed prints consumed all wall space, which was barely visible beyond the stacks and piles. Chairs provided storage for linens, pillows and heaps of clothing. Tables were buried by more glassware, books and tchotchkes. The faint scents of mildewed paper, disinfectant and stale food filled the air.

My senses could not take in all the clutter. I have never thought of myself as claustrophobic, but being there was overwhelming. I managed to chat with my friend's elderly mom and let her know I had been praying for her. And she had just found her glasses—praise You, Lord!—right before we pulled up. Relieved that his mother could see to take her medication, my friend kept our visit brief.

"I'm sorry you had to see that, Sam," he said on our drive to my office. "I can only imagine what you must be thinking."

"Buddy, there is no judgment here—you know that. That has to be so tough for you. And I certainly have a better idea of how to pray for her—and you."

"Thank you," he said. "She's gotten a lot worse since my dad died last year. He kept some kind of order even while knowing she had a problem with hoarding. Now it's almost as if she's unable to see the chaos of her big mess."

"Well, she's not the only one with that problem," I said. "We may not be hoarders, but many people remain blind to the mess they're in."

Messy Is as Messy Does

What comes to mind when you think about a messy area of your life?

For many people, I imagine their home or some part of it comes to mind. To them, messy means a physical, tangible display of random objects and disorganized debris. Simply put, things are not where they should be. I hope you do not struggle with hoarding, but I suspect we can all relate to this kind of messy at some level. At various times, most of us have had a messy garage, messy attic, messy storage room or at the very least a messy junk drawer.

Depending on the number of occupants in a home, messy can be a constant battle. It is hard to reclaim order in the midst of diverse, individual habits. Roommates must often negotiate the acceptable level of messy everyone can accept. And parents of small children know the challenge of teaching their children how to put away their toys and tidy up their rooms so that they learn how to clean up their messes.

Defining messy is usually subjective and based on your notion of how things should be organized or arranged. What is messy to someone who has OCD may seem neat and tidy to the rest of us. I have known some artistic, creative types who insisted that their cluttered desk and disheveled workspace reflected their associative way of organizing pieces of their latest innovative creation.

Then there are people like my friend's mother, who suffers from a tendency to hoard as many objects as possible. From her impaired perception, acquiring more and more possessions will somehow alleviate her grief, fear and anxiety. As my friend noted, she can no longer see the outer mess that manifests her inner turmoil and chaos.

Which brings us to the other definition of messy—the more complicated, mental, emotional, relational and situational kind of messy. Others may not be able to see this kind of messy in your life—at least, not initially. This form of messy often dwells in shadows and secrets, in shame and subversion. Messy addictions and messy affairs. Messy finances and messy parenting. Messy rumors and messy manipulations. Messy lies and messy consequences.

I suspect that the longer someone experiences a messy life on the inside, the more likely it is that this will be revealed in a messy external life. Neurologists and psychologists tell us that our brains are wired to organize all the sensory data coming in and to make sense of it by ordering it and finding patterns. This not only helps us with drawing conclusions about people but with arranging items in our kitchen.[1]

Similarly, when we live with sinful secrets, habits and relationships that go against what we know is right or what we know God has told us to do, then we experience distress. As the consequences of our choices play out, problems may snowball into an avalanche encompassing most areas of our lives. Soon we lose sight of how things should be in order to protect our secrets, to justify our sinful indulgences and to hide our mistakes.

When faced with the mess of a marriage that is shattered by adultery, or the chaos of a career that was ended by embezzlement, your dis-order and dis-ease eventually spill over, scalding and scarring those around you. This kind of messy can seem harder to clean up than the tangible kind, because it requires supernatural intervention to restore not just what you have lost, but what you did not have before.

Give Me a Drink

When Jesus healed the blind man as reported in John 9, He chose a hands-on, messy method for making a miracle. "After saying this, he spit on the ground, made some mud with the saliva, and put it on the man's eyes. 'Go,' he told him, 'wash in the Pool of Siloam' (this word means 'Sent'). So the man went and washed, and came home seeing" (John 9:6–7).

As we explored in the last chapter, He did not have to use this manner, but because we know nothing is accidental with God, Jesus definitely had His reasons. Foremost among them, I am convinced, was to illustrate His power to bless our mess into wholeness even when we cannot see the extent of our messiness, like the man who had been blind since birth. In other words, Jesus heals our vision—our ability to see our sin, our need and God's grace—even when we do not realize that we are blind.

We find this kind of restoration in another of Christ's most intriguing encounters—the Samaritan woman at the well. Leading up to their meeting, Jesus had heard that the Pharisees were grumbling about His ministry. He decided to leave Judea and return to Galilee (see John 4:1–3). Apparently, His route took Him through Samaria, where Jesus came to a town called Sychar, known historically for the piece of land Jacob had given to his favorite son, Joseph (see verse 5).

In Sychar, a spot remained known as Jacob's well, which is where Jesus paused to rest from His journey around noon (see verse 6).

Then along came a local woman intent on filling her water jugs, unaware that she had a divine appointment to keep.

> When a Samaritan woman came to draw water, Jesus said to her, "Will you give me a drink?" (His disciples had gone into the town to buy food.) The Samaritan woman said to him, "You are a Jew and I am a Samaritan woman. How can you ask me for a drink?" (For Jews do not associate with Samaritans.) Jesus answered her, "If you knew the gift of God and who it is that asks you for a drink, you would have asked him and he would have given you living water." "Sir," the woman said, "you have nothing to draw with and the well is deep. Where can you get this living water? Are you greater than our father Jacob, who gave us the well and drank from it himself, as did also his sons and his livestock?" Jesus answered, "Everyone who drinks this water will be thirsty again, but whoever drinks the water I give them will never thirst. Indeed, the water I give them will become in them a spring of water welling up to eternal life." The woman said to him, "Sir, give me this water so that I won't get thirsty and have to keep coming here to draw water." He told her, "Go, call your husband and come back." "I have no husband," she replied. Jesus said to her, "You are right when you say you have no husband. The fact is, you have had five husbands, and the man you now have is not your husband. What you have just said is quite true."
>
> John 4:7–18

Notice the poise and compassion with which Jesus engaged this woman, someone culturally considered unclean by the majority of Jewish people at the time. He began by doing the unexpected—asking her for a drink of water from the well. Immediately, her curiosity must have been piqued: *Who is this stranger violating Jewish religious customs? Why would such a man ask me for a drink?*

After she voiced her confusion, Jesus turned the tables on her. Now that He clearly had her full attention, He said, "You really should be asking me for a drink of living water to quench that insatiable thirst inside you." Basically, He used their location to craft the perfect metaphor for this woman's messy life.

Apparently, though, her confusion persisted as she began trying to understand what this mystery man could be talking about. Instead of wondering, *Why would this Jew ask me, a Samaritan, for a drink?* she asked, "How can You give me a drink when You don't have a container to hold water?" Drawing on the history of their locale, which she likely expected a Jew to know, she tried to unravel His meaning: "Are You greater than our father Jacob?"

Not only did she wonder how this man could give her a drink, but her question also implied a more urgent concern: Who are You? She realized this was no typical Jewish stranger resting beside Jacob's well.

Jesus answered her by explaining the contrast between the two kinds of water being discussed, both the literal well water and the spiritual soul water. While a drink of water from the well would only provide temporary relief to physical thirst, the water He offered her would quench her greatest need once and for all.

With that kind of offer, the woman immediately requested this life-giving water so that she would not have to keep returning to the well. In conflating the two kinds of water, though, she was still missing the point. Jesus then told her to go fetch her husband and come back, and she replied that she had no husband.

In one of the greatest examples of divine revelation, Jesus removed the blindfold from this woman's eyes. "You are right when you say you have no husband. The fact is, you have had five husbands, and the man you now have is not your husband. What you have just said is quite true." Christ dropped a bombshell, revealing that He knew all about her.

42

But He did it with great kindness. He did not call her a liar or an adulteress or even an immoral woman. Jesus simply pointed to the truth of her situation, to the factual evidence of the soul thirst that she had been trying to quench in ways that never satisfied her longing for more. He did not confront her right away or call her out on her past behavior. He made it clear that He was not there to judge her or condemn her. He was there to heal her. He was there to bless her mess.

Miracle in the Mundane

The Samaritan woman then assumed Jesus must be a prophet, to which He replied, in essence: "You're seeing more clearly, but keep looking." Then she must have had an "Aha!" moment as the stranger's identity came into full focus:

> The woman said, "I know that Messiah" (called Christ) "is coming. When he comes, he will explain everything to us." Then Jesus declared, "I, the one speaking to you—I am he." Just then his disciples returned and were surprised to find him talking with a woman. But no one asked, "What do you want?" or "Why are you talking with her?" Then, leaving her water jar, the woman went back to the town and said to the people, "Come, see a man who told me everything I ever did. Could this be the Messiah?" They came out of the town and made their way toward him.
>
> John 4:25–30

Jesus waited to confirm His identity directly until the woman arrived at the truth. Rather than announce that He was the Messiah when they first met, He demonstrated His power to see her and her need for what He offered. Jesus helped her see what she could not see in herself. And He helped her see it in a way that resulted in grace and not shame.

Not surprisingly, the disciples did not get what was going on when they returned and discovered their Master concluding His conversation with someone with whom they had been culturally conditioned to look down upon. To their credit, they did not ask the question you or I might have posed: "What are You—the holy Son of God—doing talking to her—a woman from a pagan country, with a bad reputation?"

The woman became so excited about meeting Jesus that she left her water jar at the well. We can imagine this had probably never happened before. Basically, she came there on a mundane errand in the middle of the day and left transformed by her encounter with the Messiah, the Giver of living water. Her testimony must have made quite an impression, too, because many of her neighbors from town also believed in Christ.

SHE WAS AN EVANGELIST FOR THE MESSIAH WHO HAD CHANGED HER LIFE.

No longer would she be known as a woman with questionable morals and a shady past. Now she was an evangelist for the Messiah who had changed her life.

When you encounter Jesus and drink the living water that only He gives, when you experience the ability to see clearly, your life will never be the same. He is not put off by your mess, by your past or by your inability to see yourself clearly. Jesus told His followers, "I have come that they may have life, and have it to the full" (John 10:10). And His gift of new life remains the same for us today.

The Samaritan woman could never have expected or imagined that she would encounter the Messiah, the long-awaited Son of God the prophets had been describing for the past four hundred years, on an average day doing an average chore. She had no idea that morning that her priorities were about to shift and that her relationships were about to change. She did not realize walking along the hot, dusty path to Jacob's well that she was about to encounter the living God. She could not see then what she could see after meeting Him.

Never underestimate the impact your mess-turned-miracle can have on other people. Remember that Jesus told His disciples that the blind man's limitation was not the result of his sin or the sin of his parents but rather an opportunity for God's glory to be manifest. The same is true for whatever mess you may be mired in right now. God uses our messes to get our attention as well as the attention of others. Just as we are inspired by the examples of the blind man and the Samaritan woman, other people will soon be inspired by you.

Expect Your Surprise

The blind man did not realize that he was about to receive the gift of sight from the One who had created him. He had no idea that gooey mud held together by the Master's spit would give him what he had never had before. The blind man experienced the power of Jesus through a dirty, messy mask of miraculous mud.

The Samaritan woman did not expect to see her messy life washed clean by the Messiah. She did not anticipate that a stranger could see her heart and know all about her life. She did not dare hope that a drink of well water might lead to a soul-quenching spring of eternal life.

You may not be expecting to see what God is about to do next in your life, but that does not mean you should not be ready. In fact, based on the way Jesus poured His power into those He healed and encountered, you should expect to be surprised! If you are serious about wanting to invite Jesus into your mess so that He can bless it and transform it into His miracle, then get ready.

In Jesus' name, you are about to see what you have never seen before! You are about to see it in your own life, in the lives of your family and in the lives of those around you. You are about to see

IN JESUS' NAME, YOU ARE ABOUT TO SEE WHAT YOU HAVE NEVER SEEN BEFORE!

it personally, professionally, privately and publicly. You are about to see the power of Jesus heal, transform, illuminate, save, sanctify and elevate in ways you have never witnessed. God's Word promises us, "However, as it is written: 'What no eye has seen, what no ear has heard, and what no human mind has conceived'—the things God has prepared for those who love him'" (1 Corinthians 2:9). This not only applies to what awaits you in heaven, my friend, but this applies to the miracle God has for you here on earth.

Powered by the Holy Spirit, you are about to see God work in ways that leave your eyes wide, your mouth open, your spine tingling and your heart singing. You are about to see your marriage healed, your work transformed and your health touched by the Great Physician. Just because you cannot imagine your miracle does not mean that God's power is not already in the midst of your mud. Just because there is mud in your eyes right now does not mean that you are not about to receive new vision. Just because your soul remains thirsty right now does not mean that you are not about to be quenched with the satisfaction of living water.

You are about to see what God can do when you let Him open your eyes.

You are about to see more people come to Jesus than ever before in human history.

You are about to see your prodigal sons and daughters come back home.

You are about to see your leaders serve with honesty and
   integrity.
You are about to see your community overflowing with love
   and kindness.
You are about to see your church changing the world.
You are about to see your country come together as one nation under God.

I understand if you feel skeptical or have your doubts. And I appreciate how painful your life may be right now. I can believe you
have been waiting for God to unleash His power in your life for a
long time. I do not doubt that you have been praying and praying
and have not received an answer yet.

I know that everyone around the world has been through a traumatic ordeal, both personally and globally. I know COVID is real.
My family went through it. I know millions of people still suffer its
debilitating effects. I grieve the hundreds of thousands of lives ended
by this pandemic disease. But no matter how powerful COVID or
any other illness may seem, our God will always be infinitely more
powerful.

So no matter how hard hit you have been by COVID or cancer
or diabetes or depression or anxiety, we cannot bow at their altar.
The next thing to fill our nation will not defeat us. I do not care
which variant it may be, where it originated or what its new number
is—our God is more powerful!

The next thing to fill this world will be the glory of the Risen
   Christ.
Your nation's mess is about to become God's miracle.
Your family's mess is about to become a miracle.
Your financial mess is about to become a miracle.

Your health mess is about to become a miracle.
Your legal mess is about to become a miracle.
Your emotional mess is about to become a miracle.
Your relational mess is about to become a miracle.
Your career mess is about to become a miracle.
Your worst mess is about to become your best miracle.
No matter what your mess, it is about to be blessed!

Your Joy Is Coming

Before you dismiss my prophetic declarations as unbridled optimism, know that I make them not because of who I am or what I know. I make these prophetic declarations because I know the God whose power knows no limits. I am not living in denial but in full awareness of divine deliverance. If the old saying is true, that it is darkest before the dawn, then it is no surprise everything seems messiest before it is most miraculous.

I know what you have been through. In recent years we have seen darkness. We have seen world events transpire that we have never seen before. We have seen the ruins of what once was.

The ruins of this global pandemic.

The ruins of racial and social unrest destroying property, fragmenting families, dividing communities and shattering the Church.

The ruins of political unrest where the donkey and the elephant temporarily succeed in dividing what belongs to the Lamb.

The ruins of a cancel culture that insists on silencing everyone and everything that refuses to toe the line of a morally relativistic ideological worldview that runs counter to the Word and the Spirit of God.

The ruins of secular totalitarianism that explicitly states casinos and liquor stores are essential but the Church is not.

The ruins of a generation targeted by the architects of darkness with the message that there is no such thing as truth, gender, holiness and personal responsibility.

The ruins of a life that you struggle to enjoy because you are overwhelmed by the pressing demands pulling you in every direction.

The ruins of dreams you once pursued with energy and excitement only to watch them dwindle to cold ashes of disappointment and regret.

We see these ruins. And we have wept from the depths of these ruins. But our tears are not in vain. Because God's Word promises, "Weeping may stay for the night, but rejoicing comes in the morning" (Psalm 30:5). My friend, our joy is coming. A new day is dawning. Night is coming to an end. It may be dark right now, but the sunshine brings new joy!

OPEN YOUR EYES TO THE POWER OF JESUS CHRIST IN YOUR LIFE.

No matter what your mess looks like, no matter how much damage it has done in your life and the lives of those you love, and no matter how desperate you may feel, open your eyes to the power of Jesus Christ in your life. Invite Him in to play in the mud at your feet. Meet Him at the old well and let Him see you right where you are. Ask the Holy Spirit to give you eyes to see what you have never seen before.

And in order for us to see what we have never seen before, it behooves us to reconcile our eschatology with our missiology. In other words, I do believe Jesus is coming to unleash His power as never before. But permit me to remind you:

He is not coming back for a broken Church.
He is not coming back for a whining Church.
He is not coming back for a depressed Church.

He is not coming back for a fearful Church.

He is not coming back for a defeated Church.

He is not coming back for a politically correct Church.

He is not coming back for a comfortable Church.

He is not coming back for a silent Church.

He is not coming back for a dying Church.

Jesus Christ is coming back for a glorious Church,

A triumphant Church,

A thriving Church,

A victorious Church,

A holy Church.

And while we are waiting for Jesus to come down, Jesus is waiting for us to stand up! Are you ready to see what we have never seen before? Allow me to give you a preview of what we are about to see in the Spirit:

Instead of riots, revival.

Instead of lockdowns, open heavens.

Instead of strife, unity.

Instead of hatred, love.

Instead of relativism, truth.

Instead of destroying property, building altars.

Instead of confrontation, conversations.

Instead of political affiliations, prophetic designations.

Instead of many under fear, one nation under God.

You are about to see what you have never seen before.

Look with wonder as the power of Christ radically transforms your life.

——— OPEN YOUR EYES ———

Once again, here are some questions to assist you in applying this chapter's biblical truths and prophetic promises. Please do not allow this to become a burden or obligation. Consider, instead, that it is an additional opportunity to draw closer to Jesus as you experience more of His miraculous healing power in your life. Reflecting on your responses to these questions is beneficial, but you will discover more lasting change if you write down your thoughts so that you can return to them later for further contemplation.

As before, I have also provided a brief prayer to help begin your time of intimacy with God concerning all you are learning in these pages. Simply take a few moments in stillness and silence before the Lord to quiet your mind and unburden your heart before Him. Remember, Jesus is right there with you amid your mess, waiting to bless you, heal you and transform you.

1. What areas of your life seem particularly messy to you right now? What do you believe is causing or contributing to your messes? Which mess preoccupies most of your time and energy at present?

2. What are some ways you feel like the Samaritan woman at the well? What is your deepest longing or greatest spiritual thirst right now?

3. When have you seen the power of Jesus make an important difference in your life? Where do you want to see His power unleashed in your life next? Why?

Dear Lord, thank You that I am about to see what I have never seen before. I trust You and claim Your promise of abundant life in all areas of my life. In my family, in my faith, in my finances, in my relationships, in my Church, in my community, in my thinking, in my actions, in my words, in my attitude, in my health, in my surroundings, in my nation and in my generation. Quench my thirst for Your miraculous presence in my life. Allow me to drink deeply from the living water You provide. Give me patience as Your Spirit continues to transform me into the image of Christ. In Jesus' name, Amen.

Fresh Perspective

*Open Your Eyes to What You
Have Been Missing*

Our God is not only the God of messy miracles.
Our God is a God who satisfies our deepest longings.

Sometimes what we have been looking for is right in front of us.

If you are like me, you have probably had moments when you cannot find your glasses, keys or phone only to discover that they are on your face, in your ignition or in your pocket. We often become so busy and distracted by the demands of our day that we lose sight of the little items we have come to depend on. We rush from home to work or school to appointments and then back home again, often so focused on the future that we lose sight of the present. We get so distracted that we do not see what is in front of us or pay attention to our own actions.

I suspect we experience a similar kind of blurred perspective in our spiritual lives. How often do we realize that our longing for more of God in our lives is already present and available? We miss out on seeing what we have in the present because we are living conditionally in the future. We assume that we will have more power, more peace, more joy and purpose someday when we are more spiritually mature. But often we are waiting on God to move in our lives, to answer our prayers or to reveal our next steps when God is waiting on us to see what is right in front of us. When we are willing to open our eyes spiritually, we see that God has already given us all we need and more.

Now You See Me

Sometimes we fail to see what God is doing in our lives because we rely on what others think of us. Even when they realize there is something different about us due to God's presence, we may try to convince them that we are just like them, the same person we have always been.

After Jesus healed the man who had been blind since birth, others did not recognize him:

His neighbors and those who had formerly seen him begging asked, "Isn't this the same man who used to sit and beg?" Some claimed that he was. Others said, "No, he only looks like him." But he himself insisted, "I am the man." "How then were your eyes opened?" they asked. He replied, "The man they call Jesus made some mud and put it on my eyes. He told me to go to Siloam and wash. So I went and washed, and then I could see." "Where is this man?" they asked him. "I don't know," he said.

John 9:8–12

Notice the man's neighbors tried to talk themselves out of the truth of what they saw by assuming it was just coincidental resemblance. They had grown accustomed to perceiving this man based only on his lack of sight. Perhaps he usually sat and begged at a certain location near the temple, and that is the only context they had for who he was and what he was about. He was simply the blind man who begged, someone they dismissed as irrelevant to their lives.

Even as they struggled to accept the miracle that occurred in this man's life, he insisted that he was still the same guy. He then explained matter-of-factly how Jesus had gone about healing him, which likely sounded a bit strange, to say the least. Because then the people asked, "Well, where is this man who healed you?" to which the man replied, "I don't know." The blind man testified to the truth of the messy miracle that had just transformed his life, but he likely was still processing the implications. Remember, he had been blind since birth, so every color, shape, face and landscape must have overwhelmed him with unfamiliar visual data. Then to have his neighbors practically not recognize him on top of it all. Despite being able to see, this man was no longer who he used to be—yet who had he become?

Sometimes we get so familiar with someone, including ourselves, in a certain location that we lose sight of them as an actual human being. They become part of the landscape—the barista at our coffee shop, the homeless person on the corner, the clerk in the convenience store, the receptionist at our doctor's office. With repeated viewings over time, they are seen and identified by others only by association of what they do in a particular locale at a particular time. For those who pass them every day, their identity does not exist outside of that time and place.

Until something changes and they are forced to see others in a different light.

Can I Take Your Order?

When our kids were young, I picked them up from school one day when Eva, my wife, was unable to be there. Seizing the out-of-the-ordinary opportunity with me chauffeuring them, the kids begged to stop at McDonald's for a snack. I agreed to go with the flow of making it a special occasion. When I saw the drive-thru backed up by others with the same great idea, I figured it would likely be faster to go inside to order. The restaurant was less crowded inside, so we got in line.

After a couple minutes, it was finally our turn.

Just as I was about to order two kids' meals and an apple pie, I heard, "Oh! Pastor Sam! Is that you? Wow, what are you doing here?" The wide-eyed young lady who had asked the questions attended our church.

I recognized her and said, "Hey! How are you? Just being Dad today and let the kids twist my arm for a snack after school. We'll have—"

"Sorry," she interrupted. "It's just that I don't usually see many people I know. And, well, I only see you at church. I thought it was you, but then I just never thought about you eating at McDonald's, you know?"

I chuckled. "Yes, I love a Big Mac as much as anyone else! I've been known to eat at Burger King, too—and even Taco Bell—but don't tell anyone." Her eyes widened even more—I had clearly blown her mind! "You know I'm just teasing, right? I mean, I do eat fast food sometimes."

"Right, of course," she said, still processing that her pastor was in a McDonald's with his kids. "What can I get you?"

By this time, my son and daughter were giggling and could not stop. They thought it was hilarious that this young lady was confused by my presence in a place in which she was not used to seeing me. Being the inherent teacher at heart that I am, I tried to explain to them about context and how we see people. Perhaps they did not fully understand what I meant, but I trust that you get my point and have probably had a similar experience.

SEEING IS ABOUT MUCH MORE THAN WHAT IS BEFORE OUR EYES.

Because seeing is about much more than what is before our eyes. Who we are is much more than the roles we play. Once we experience miraculous power in our messes, we are never the same.

Blinded by the Light

When you encounter the sight-giving, life-changing and heart-transforming power of Jesus, you are no longer who you once were. Others may not recognize you because your attitude, speech and behavior changes, sometimes dramatically. The thoughts and activities that once held your attention no longer matter when your focus shifts to knowing the Lord and living by His Spirit. God's Word tells us, "Therefore, if anyone is in Christ, he is a new creation; old things have passed away; behold, all things have become new" (2 Corinthians 5:17 NKJV).

Once you give your life to Christ and the Holy Spirit dwells in you, you see things differently. Old pursuits and idolatrous habits lose their power over you. You realize that some relationships that once sustained you were actually holding you back. Your eyes become focused on an eternal perspective that glorifies God and advances His Kingdom.

One of the best and most dramatic examples of a before-and-after transformation in the Bible occurred in the life of the apostle Paul. Previously known as Saul, he not only did not know Christ, but he actively persecuted followers of Jesus, determined to use violence or whatever means necessary to prevent them from spreading the Gospel. Saul had been raised in a strict household that conditioned him in the rigid legalism of Jewish religious practices.

Based on his allegiance to traditional Judaism, Saul apparently considered Jesus to be a dangerous heretic and His followers just as harmful to the Jewish faith. Then one day while traveling to Damascus in hopes of capturing and arresting more followers of the Way, Saul was literally stopped in his tracks:

> As he neared Damascus on his journey, suddenly a light from heaven flashed around him. He fell to the ground and heard a voice say to him, "Saul, Saul, why do you persecute me?" "Who are you, Lord?" Saul asked. "I am Jesus, whom you are persecuting," he replied. "Now get up and go into the city, and you will be told what you must do." The men traveling with Saul stood there speechless; they heard the sound but did not see anyone. Saul got up from the ground, but when he opened his eyes he could see nothing. So they led him by the hand into Damascus. For three days he was blind, and did not eat or drink anything.
>
> Acts 9:3–9

While Saul physically could see, he failed to realize the truth that Jesus was the Messiah, the Son of God come to earth in human form. How ironic then that Saul's encounter with Christ leaves the bounty hunter blind, which finally parallels the spiritual state in which he had been living. Saul's blindness also forced him to come to terms with what he had been missing. Notice that Jesus asks him, "Why are you persecuting Me?" Implicit in this question is another, more personal one: "Why can't you see who I am? Why are you blind to the truth?"

It is the same question Jesus continues to ask us today, even after we have invited Him into our lives. Sometimes when we live in shadows, we are initially blinded by the power of God's light. Just as our physical eyes adjust as our pupils constrict in bright light, we discover we must adjust our vision spiritually.

Sharp Focus

As the blinded Saul was led to Damascus, he must have been in shock. In a matter of moments, his entire life had been turned upside down. One minute, he has focused on rounding up a subversive group of renegades who were violating Jewish laws and traditions. With his rage channeled into dogged determination, Saul was evidently good at his job of capturing Christ-followers. Because when God directed one of the believers in Damascus, a man named Ananias, to lay hands on Saul so that his conversion might be complete, Ananias balked. "'Lord,' Ananias answered, 'I have heard many reports about this man and all the harm he has done to your holy people in Jerusalem. And he has come here with authority from the chief priests to arrest all who call on your name'" (Acts 9:13–14).

While Ananias had never met Saul, he had no desire to do so based on Saul's reputation. Apparently, Saul's name struck fear in the hearts of believers because his passion for thwarting them was so intense. If we put ourselves in Ananias's place, the situation appeared as if it might be a setup. What if Saul was pretending in order to draw out believers and arrest them? A logical, cautionary question from a human perspective, but God made it explicitly clear to Ananias. "Go! This man is my chosen instrument to proclaim my name to the Gentiles and their kings and to the people of Israel. I will show him how much he must suffer for my name" (Acts 9:15–16).

When we are learning to see spiritually, we must trust God and step out in faith. Ananias placed his faith in God and obeyed His instructions rather than succumbing to the fear produced by his human perspective. Saul was about to do the same and take his first baby step of faith as a believer. God was not only restoring Saul's physical sight; He was also opening the eyes of Saul's heart with the power of the Holy Spirit:

> Then Ananias went to the house and entered it. Placing his hands on Saul, he said, "Brother Saul, the Lord—Jesus, who appeared to you on the road as you were coming here—has sent me so that you may see again and be filled with the Holy Spirit." Immediately, something like scales fell from Saul's eyes, and he could see again. He got up and was baptized, and after taking some food, he regained his strength.
>
> Acts 9:17–19

We see that Saul's transformation, both physically and spiritually, had been made complete. Once again, notice how God used this situation to strengthen the faith of Ananias while transforming Saul. Ananias placed his hands on this man who was known to be an enemy of the Gospel. He relayed the message that Jesus had sent him so that Saul could see again and be filled with the Spirit. While Ananias could already see spiritually, surely the miracle transpiring before him must have brought the power of God into sharp focus.

Watch Where You Are Going

Without a doubt, at least from a spiritual perspective, Saul's life was a mess. He not only failed to see the truth of Christ in his own life, but he was committed to eradicating this truth in the lives of others. Basically, Saul worked for the enemy by persecuting believers and trying to prevent the Good News of the Gospel from spreading. But where Saul thought he was going was not where the apostle we know as Paul ended up going.

Immediately after being filled with the Holy Spirit, Saul began doing what must have been unthinkable and unimaginable only days earlier: preaching the Gospel of grace through the power of Jesus of Nazareth. We are told Saul spent several days with the other believers in Damascus and wasted no time doing what he had originally come there to prevent:

> At once he began to preach in the synagogues that Jesus is the Son of God. All those who heard him were astonished and asked, "Isn't he the man who raised havoc in Jerusalem among those who call on this name? And hasn't he come here to take them as prisoners to the chief priests?" Yet Saul grew more and more powerful and baffled the Jews living in Damascus by proving that Jesus is the Messiah.
>
> Acts 9:20–22

If someone had told Saul, the Jewish zealot who lived to persecute Christians, the incredible impact he would have on spreading the Gospel of Jesus Christ, he would never have believed them. But such is the power of God in our lives to do what we ourselves could never do on our own. So often we think we know what we are doing and how we will do it. We rely on human logic and probability, interpreting our perceptions to see only what we want to see while remaining blind to the power of God's truth in our lives.

When we are filled with the Spirit, we surrender our own agendas, schedules and itineraries in order to go where He directs when

He wants us to go. Many times, when we allow the Spirit to guide us, we find ourselves outside of our comfort zones and inside of God's incredible plan for our lives. While we usually want to know where we are going and what to expect, God's plan transcends the route we would choose. James warns us:

> Now listen, you who say, "Today or tomorrow we will go to this or that city, spend a year there, carry on business and make money." Why, you do not even know what will happen tomorrow. What is your life? You are a mist that appears for a little while and then vanishes. Instead, you ought to say, "If it is the Lord's will, we will live and do this or that."
>
> James 4:13–15

Seeing clearly from God's perspective means trusting Him to lead the way.

You Will Know It When You See It

When we become blinded to the power of God within us, we often look for fulfillment elsewhere, usually in some sinful pursuit that provides temporary pleasure or a sense of power over our lives. Saul believed that by following all the rules of the Law of Moses according to Jewish traditions, he was a righteous man. Those who refused to follow these laws and customs because of the freedom they found in Jesus clearly enraged Saul because these believers threatened his self-justifying system. He had to encounter Christ and experience physical blindness in order to overcome the spiritual blindness that was his central problem.

Although most of us do not lose our physical vision when our spiritual vision is obscured, we nonetheless experience blindness.

Perhaps we fail to see the truth about a relationship that is harming us, and we convince ourselves to remain in a dangerous situation. We might go deeper in debt rather than seeing the harsh truth about the state of our finances. We might be in denial about our physical health or the impact of a lingering trauma in our lives. We see what we want to see and refuse to see the truth of our situation, factually as well as spiritually.

Often when we are blinding ourselves to the truth, we fixate on something we believe will fulfill us. If this relationship did not work out, maybe the next one will. If the problem is spending, then more money is bound to help. If our body causes us pain, then medication or alcohol can dull our senses and lessen our suffering. Eventually, however, we realize that we can only ignore what we have refused to see for so long. Then the truth, one way or another, opens our eyes to what we have been missing.

Jesus often told parables to illustrate His teaching, and perhaps none exemplifies our human attempts to find what we are missing as poignantly as the tale of a father and his two sons. While the younger son, or prodigal as he is often called, had eyes with pupils, irises and retinas that functioned normally, he suffered acute blindness regarding what he really wanted most in life. Apparently, he felt as if he was missing something that would satisfy him more than life at home. I doubt he even knew what it was, but he assumed he would know it when he saw it.

Blinded by Desire

Whether he was bored or arrogant or simply immature, or some hybrid of these variables and others, the younger son refused to see a future that required him to postpone the life he thought he wanted. "'Father, give me my share of the estate.' So he divided his

63

property between them" (Luke 15:12). But I daresay the younger son did not experience the fulfillment he had likely envisioned:

> "Not long after that, the younger son got together all he had, set off for a distant country and there squandered his wealth in wild living. After he had spent everything, there was a severe famine in that whole country, and he began to be in need. So he went and hired himself out to a citizen of that country, who sent him to his fields to feed pigs. He longed to fill his stomach with the pods that the pigs were eating, but no one gave him anything."
>
> Luke 15:13–16

This young man could only see a future in which he enjoyed what he knew would one day be his. He figured, "Why wait?" and had the audacity to ask his father to give him his inheritance right away. Keep in mind this was essentially telling his father, "I wish you were dead. Getting your money now is more important to me than our relationship." Either the younger son failed to see the impact his selfish request would have on his father and their relationship or he simply did not care. Regardless, the younger son was a blind man.

Blinded by his own desires for adventure, excitement and pleasure, the young man discovered that getting what you want only provides a temporary hit of what it is you truly long for. We can never sustain our blindness to what is true about us, true about God and true about our need for God. Nothing we pursue—money, houses, clothes, jewelry, possessions, achievements, beauty, celebrity, social media fame, *nothing*—satisfies the spiritual craving we have for the presence of God's Holy Spirit in our lives.

The young man spent all of his inheritance and found himself impoverished at the worst possible time—in the midst of a famine.

He had failed to look ahead and prepare for adversity, and he had severed relationships with his family. But when he could no longer sustain the illusion, when he had squandered his money and hit rock bottom and when he was alone at the pig trough, the metaphorical scales fell from his eyes.

Come to Your Senses

Once he could no longer sustain his blindness, the young man found himself humbled by his own choices. There was no one to blame but himself, but facing the truth without blinders required experiencing the pain, regret and loneliness of his dire situation. But even in the midst of such emotional, physical and spiritual turmoil, the young man saw something else that was unmistakably true:

> "*When he came to his senses*, he said, 'How many of my father's hired servants have food to spare, and here I am starving to death! I will set out and go back to my father and say to him: Father, I have sinned against heaven and against you. I am no longer worthy to be called your son; make me like one of your hired servants.' So he got up and went to his father."
>
> Luke 15:17–20, emphasis added

I love that phrase: "when he came to his senses." How perfectly it expresses the "Aha!" moment we experience when we see the truth and realize what we have been missing, denying or ignoring. Like waking from a bad dream, the young man gained crystal clarity of himself and his situation. He could no longer pretend to be the party-loving vagabond who was only out for a good time. He could no longer escape the consequences of his actions. The prodigal son hit his lowest point and looked at life from the bottom of a pig pail. But as he came to his senses, that vantage point broke through his blindness.

Are there areas of your life in which you need to come to your senses? When you are challenged by a tough day, how do you respond?

Do you demand your inheritance right away and feel entitled to find relief through a harmful habit, an old addiction or a temporary pleasure? Do you prop up the image of yourself that you want others to see rather than the weak, impoverished person you are in that moment? Do you envy what others have and assume their happiness can only be found in your own pursuits?

IT IS TIME TO OPEN YOUR EYES. Not easy questions to answer, my friend, but it is time to open your eyes to what you have been missing. It is time to see what God wants to do in your life. Whether you have strayed from God and know it is time to come home, or you have been blinded by the distractions and demands of life, it is time to open your eyes.

Drop the Blindfold

When the prodigal son opened his eyes, he might have been surprised, much as Saul was surprised by what he experienced, or as the blind man healed by Jesus was surprised. Humbled and finally aware of what he had been missing, the young man must have wondered if his eyes were playing tricks on him:

> "But while he was still a long way off, his father saw him and was filled with compassion for him; he ran to his son, threw his arms around him and kissed him. The son said to him, 'Father, I have sinned against heaven and against you. I am no longer worthy to be called your son.' But the father said to his servants, 'Quick! Bring

the best robe and put it on him. Put a ring on his finger and sandals on his feet. Bring the fattened calf and kill it. Let's have a feast and celebrate. For this son of mine was dead and is alive again; he was lost and is found.' So they began to celebrate."

Luke 15:20–24

When we look for power, purpose and peace in anything other than God, we underestimate all that He has for us. When we grow impatient and demand our inheritance right now rather than trusting patiently and waiting on the Lord, we overlook the abundance of blessings ahead of us. When we finally open our eyes to what we have been missing, we realize that God comes running to shower us with His lavish love. He not only welcomes us home with grace and forgiveness, but He celebrates us with His extravagant blessings.

Too often we expect judgment and condemnation rather than grace and mercy. Too often we accept depression and despair rather than joy and peace. Too often we settle for less than the portion God wants to give us.

We blindfold ourselves with negativity, worry, stress, anger and anxiety rather than open our eyes to the power of the Spirit in us. We chase after what cannot satisfy us and grow weary from our efforts. We fight battles we know we cannot win and wonder why we already feel defeated; however, when we open our eyes to God's miracle in our mess, we realize that our battles belong to Him. In fact, they have already been won by Him through the victory of the resurrection.

When the people of Israel felt outnumbered and overwhelmed by the armies of their adversaries, they allowed their fear to blind them. Surrounded by stronger, bigger, better-equipped foes, the Israelites looked left and right but forgot to look up. But let me tell you the same thing God told His people in those moments, "Do not be afraid or discouraged because of this vast army. For the battle is not yours, but God's" (2 Chronicles 20:15). In other words, He has got this!

Will you look up and let God win the battles you have been fighting? Will you allow Jesus to open your eyes? Will you let the scales blinding your vision fall to the ground so that you can see clearly once again? Will you welcome a fresh encounter with the Holy Spirit so that you can experience all you have been missing? It is time to drop the blindfolds that have been blocking your vision.

Drop the blindfold of fear.
Drop the blindfold of worry.
Drop the blindfold of doubt.
Drop the blindfold of depression.
Drop the blindfold of anxiety.
Drop the blindfold of illness.
Drop the blindfold of bankruptcy.
Drop the blindfold of breaking up.
Drop the blindfold of brokenness.

Refuse to let anything prevent you from seeing all that the Lord has for you. If it is not holy, you do not want it. If it is not blessed, you do not need it. If it is not going to give God all the glory, then you do not desire any part of it.

It is time to remove the blinders of things God never meant for you to wear. He wants you to open your eyes to all you have been missing. The Holy Spirit wants to open your eyes to the eternal perspective of life everlasting. Consider what Paul, the same man who was once Saul, wrote to his brothers and sisters in Christ at the church in Rome: "Now if we are children, then we are heirs—heirs of God and co-heirs with Christ, if indeed we share in his sufferings in order that we may also share in his glory" (Romans 8:17). Open your eyes to the reality of being a child of the King, a co-heir with Jesus Christ.

Open your eyes to healing.

Open your eyes to abundance.

Open your eyes to contentment.

Open your eyes to purpose.

Open your eyes to making a difference.

Open your eyes to joy!

OPEN YOUR EYES

By this time, you know that the following questions are provided to help you process and apply the truths shared in this chapter. Read them slowly and thoughtfully and allow the Holy Spirit to open your eyes to the truth you need to see right now. Consider where you have been allowing other people, circumstances or your own emotions to blind you to the reality of who you are in Christ.

The brief prayer below is once again offered as a way to start your conversation with God about all you are learning and experiencing right now. Take a few minutes and still your heart before Him, listening to the voice of the Spirit and the truth of His Word that comes to mind. Ask the Lord to open your eyes to all you have been missing and looking for elsewhere.

1. How does the way you see yourself often prevent you from experiencing the truth of your identity in Christ? When has the way others see you influenced you to see yourself differently?

2. Do you identify more with the blindness of self-righteousness Saul/Paul experienced or the blindness of selfish desire displayed by the prodigal son? How do you see evidence of this kind of blindness in your life right now?

3. What has God been revealing to you as He opens your eyes with the presence of His Spirit inside

you? What miracle is currently in progress in the messy parts of your life?

Dear Lord, please forgive me for the times when I have looked for fulfillment in anything other than You. I repent and turn away from my self-imposed blindness so that I can see clearly and receive the blessings You want to give. Take away all the obstacles that prevent me from seeing who You are and how You are at work in my life. Show me where You want me to step out in faith, and give me the strength through Your Spirit to take the first step. Thank You, God, for continuing to produce Your miracle out of my messiness. In Jesus' name, Amen.

Holy Spit

Open Your Eyes to God's Spirit

Do not mistake your dirty process for God's cleansing promise.
You do not have Christ's spit—you have His Spirit!

When I think of saliva, I think of DNA.

Perhaps it is because saliva is often used by doctors and scientists to discover a human being's genetic profile. While almost any human cell could be used to map someone's DNA, saliva is quick, easy and painless to submit. DNA, or deoxyribonucleic acid, the biochemical name for the molecule that carries genetic programming for anything living, is much more complex. Consisting of two strands wound around each other in a double helix, the DNA molecule in humans contains 23 pairs of chromosomes for a total of 46.[1]

You may recall from your biology classes in school that Francis Crick and James Watson are usually credited with identifying and unlocking the secrets of DNA. While their work is instrumental, a Swiss doctor working some eighty years earlier first identified the "building blocks" of life, which he called "nuclein."[2] You might remember a monk named Gregor Mendel and the experiments he did with pea plants to determine what he called recessive and dominant hereditary traits. Since then, the science of genetics continues to reveal new insight into the human body, individual preferences and family dynamics over generations.

With more revelations by researchers, the popularity of genealogy and ancestral research only continues to climb. People inherently like to know where they came from and how past generations led to their birth. Simply put, we want to know how we got here and how we belong. Thanks to advances in genetics (the branch of biology that is focused on genes and heredity) and the digitalization of archival material, we can know more about our family's origins, ethnicity and generational journeys than ever before.

Mainstream companies now offer direct-to-consumer genetic testing so that individuals can discover their ancestral composition as well as gene-related health conditions and predispositions. Most of these businesses require customers to submit a saliva sample that will then be tested and analyzed. Results allow customers to trace their roots on family trees going back hundreds of years. This knowledge can help prevent diseases and can help people prepare for hereditary conditions such as diabetes and certain cancers.

While DNA continues to reveal more and more about human beings, there is one thing it can never reflect: the spiritual condition of the heart. To reveal that need and, more importantly, the only solution, it takes more than spit.

It takes *Spirit*.

Divine DNA

When you consider the study of DNA, you may not think about one of Jesus' messiest miracles, but it does play a crucial role, nonetheless. You see, the way Jesus chose to heal the man who was blind from birth was both intimate and unexpected. Christ did not simply lay hands on the blind man. The Son of God connected His humanity to the man's calamity.

Jesus transferred something inside Himself to heal someone with an external need obvious to everyone around him. "Then he spit on the ground, made mud with the saliva, and spread the mud over the blind man's eyes" (John 9:6 NLT). Christ did not simply choose to heal this man—He literally gave the blind man part of Himself so that the man might receive something he had lacked since birth. Jesus gave this man His divine DNA.

Even if the disciples expected Jesus to heal this man of his blindness, I suspect even they were surprised by their Master's method. Spitting, the act of expelling saliva or something from one's mouth, was probably a personal habit, then as now, that one did not do publicly. Not only did He spit on the ground, but Jesus used His saliva to make a mud paste that He then smeared over the blind man's non-functioning eyes. There is no way around the obvious here: Spit and mud are, well, dirty. Grimy. Grubby. Earthy. Basic.

But could there be a better metaphor for the way Jesus continues to restore our sight today? **SOMETIMES** The unorthodox method He used to facilitate a **THE PROCESS** miracle reflects His willingness to enter into the **IS MESSY.** messiness, the murkiness and the muddiness of our lives. Sometimes the process is messy. Sometimes the process is complicated. Sometimes we get dirty from living life before we get clean from the Giver of eternal life.

Even after we come to know the Lord, we often fall into old habits and thought patterns that leave us even more vulnerable to the enemy's temptations and snares. Whether it is gossiping about those we dislike at work, cheating on our financial reports, lying to our loved ones, idolizing social media or giving in to illicit behavior, we know we are not doing what God wants us to do. Instead of living by His guidelines and the power of His Holy Spirit, we try to go our own way.

The results eventually catch up with us, though. While we feel guilty as the Spirit convicts our conscience, we may get mired in shame that only pulls us deeper into pain, regret and sinful pleasures. So we try harder. We may even experience a little progress, until life closes in on us again. Bills stack up. Harsh words pierce our heart. Family members betray us. Then we feel weak and crave immediate comfort, some way to escape our pain and misery.

Sinking deeper in the blindness of our sinful choices and consequences, we want to see again but are not sure how. As the apostle Paul described, "For I know that good itself does not dwell in me, that is, in my sinful nature. For I have the desire to do what is good, but I cannot carry it out. For I do not do the good I want to do, but the evil I do not want to do—this I keep on doing" (Romans 7:18–19).

Thanks be to God that we have a Savior who has never been afraid to get dirty!

Sent for Sinners

Jesus was not only undeterred and unafraid of getting dirty, but He was also known for hanging around people who had less-than-spotless reputations. Christ was not worried about what others might say about Him, perhaps especially when it came to the sinners with whom He associated. In fact, some of them actually became His disciples, which certainly caused quite a stir with religious leaders who considered themselves more righteous than others:

> As Jesus went on from there, he saw a man named Matthew sitting at the tax collector's booth. "Follow me," he told him, and Matthew got up and followed him. While Jesus was having dinner at Matthew's house, many tax collectors and sinners came and ate with him and his disciples. When the Pharisees saw this, they asked his disciples, "Why does your teacher eat with tax collectors and sinners?" On hearing this, Jesus said, "It is not the healthy who need a doctor, but the sick. But go and learn what this means: 'I desire mercy, not sacrifice.' For I have not come to call the righteous, but sinners."
>
> Matthew 9:9–13

Keep in mind that tax collectors during this time were often considered unscrupulous, greedy and dishonest. They would collect as much as possible from citizens, turn in the least amount acceptable to the Roman government and Jewish officials and then keep the rest for themselves. Apparently, lying and stealing came with the job for many tax collectors. The fact that Jesus would ask Matthew to follow Him was in itself scandalous. But then to eat dinner at Matthew's house with other tax collectors and assorted sinners was unimaginable.

When the Pharisees asked Jesus' disciples why the man claiming to be the Messiah would do such an unholy act, they received an answer from Jesus Himself, who had overheard them. He told them that He was not there for the righteous, for those spiritually healthy, but for sinners, those who had the sickness of sin in their souls. In other words, Jesus told them He was there to get dirty.

His response to them resonates with the answer Jesus gave to His disciples when they saw the blind man and asked, "Rabbi, who sinned, this man or his parents, that he was born blind?" (John 9:2). Their question most likely was not mean-spirited or unwarranted. In the Jewish world of the law, most matters of sin were identified by external appearances and behaviors rather than thoughts in the mind and attitudes in the heart. This system conditioned religious leaders to focus only on their public behavior, not their private words and deeds.

But this legalistic system provided no excuse for their sinful ways. God has always been concerned foremost with what is in our hearts. When He was instructing the prophet Samuel to anoint the next king of Israel, God stated, "For the LORD sees not as man sees: man looks on the outward appearance, but the LORD looks on the heart" (1 Samuel 16:7 ESV).

This interior spiritual focus also explains why Jesus repeatedly rebuked the Pharisees and Sadducees for their hypocrisy. The double standard of their hypocrisy is aptly illustrated by the problem with a dirty dish:

> "Woe to you, teachers of the law and Pharisees, you hypocrites! You clean the outside of the cup and dish, but inside they are full of greed and self-indulgence. Blind Pharisee! First clean the inside of the cup and dish, and then the outside also will be clean."
>
> Matthew 23:25–26

Jesus made it clear that we must begin from the inside out, with our hearts. Going through the motions of righteous behavior, as difficult as it may be, will always be easier than confessing the truth of our sinful hearts before God and others and receiving forgiveness and mercy. Fittingly enough, Jesus is the only way we can cleanse our hearts and follow through with our actions. Which brings us back to His answer to the disciples' question about a causal correlation between sin and the blind man's condition. "Neither this man nor his parents sinned," said Jesus, "but this happened so that the works of God might be displayed in him" (John 9:3).

Jesus Christ shines with God's grace for the glory of His Father.

Grounded by Grace

This pattern of seeking out and interacting with social outcasts and disreputable people continued throughout Jesus' ministry. In addition to Matthew, Christ also encountered a woman who had "lived a sinful life" (Luke 7:37), most likely including prostitution, a Samaritan woman with five husbands and a lover (see John 4:1–26) and Zacchaeus, a wealthy tax collector (see Luke 19:1–10). One of Christ's most dramatic encounters, however, occurred when the Jewish religious leaders dragged a woman before Him who had been caught in adultery.

> At dawn he appeared again in the temple courts, where all the people gathered around him, and he sat down to teach them. The teachers of the law and the Pharisees brought in a woman caught in adultery. They made her stand before the group and said to Jesus, "Teacher, this woman was caught in the act of adultery. In the Law Moses commanded us to stone such women. Now what do you say?" They were using this question as a trap, in order to have a basis for accusing him. But Jesus bent down and started to write on the ground with his finger. When they kept on questioning him, he straightened up and said to them, "Let any one of you who is without sin be the first to throw a stone at her." Again he stooped down and wrote on the ground. At this, those who heard began to go away one at a time, the older ones first, until only Jesus was left,

with the woman still standing there. Jesus straightened up and asked her, "Woman, where are they? Has no one condemned you?" "No one, sir," she said. "Then neither do I condemn you," Jesus declared. "Go now and leave your life of sin."

John 8:2–11

Notice the trap these religious legalists set for Christ. They wanted to see if or how Jesus, who was known for teaching mercy and grace, would dispense the Law of Moses, which required the woman to be stoned to death. If He did, then Christ would be breaking Roman law by advocating murder. Surely they must have thought they had Jesus cornered without any way out. One way or another, they would get Him. In response, however, Jesus remained silent. He stooped to write in the dust with His finger.

When the leaders kept heckling Him for an answer, Jesus turned the tables on them as only He could. Basically, He told them, "Okay. Go ahead and punish her. But only those who are without sin may throw stones." Then He wrote in the dirt once again. Christ spoke an answer that was sandwiched in between whatever He wrote on the ground, which is not revealed to us. Some scholars speculate that perhaps Jesus wrote out the accusers' names and their secret sins. Others wonder if perhaps Christ might have been providing a visual aid for His point that everyone has dirt, or sin, in their lives.

Regardless of what Jesus wrote on the ground, He used the same dust to create mud for the blind man. He showed His awareness of how all human beings bear the dirty stain of sin, which is, in fact, why Christ came. His response to the religious leaders not only avoided their devious trap, but He demonstrated the perfect balance between justice and mercy, between punishment and grace. This is the truth we see revealed elsewhere in the New Testament: "For all have sinned and fall short of the glory of God, and all are justified freely by his grace through the redemption that came by Christ Jesus" (Romans 3:23–24).

Rather than stone this woman with the Law, Jesus grounded her in His grace.

Divinity Now Accessible

When Jesus used His holy spit, His divine DNA, to make mud for a miracle, He reminded us to focus on the perfection of His promise, not the messiness of His method. The process is temporary while the promise is permanent. While the God of the outcome is the same God of the process, we often get so blinded by our pain, disappointment, anger and grief that we become disoriented about what is true. We start to confuse what we are going through with where we are going to.

I know life can be hard, brutal even. We live in a world that seems to have spun off its axis, leaving collateral damage of pandemics and pandemonium left and right. Rent goes up, gas prices go up and cost of living goes up while our paycheck does well to stay the same. Loved ones struggle, and their struggles hurt our hearts. Adult children stray from home and turn from the Lord, and our pain multiplies. Worry, anxiety, depression and uncertainty often take turns overwhelming us on an hourly basis.

But no matter what you are going through, my friend, please permit me to remind you that your temporary has run its course while your permanent is just getting started. Because if you are going through what you have never experienced before, it is only because you are about to step into what you have never stepped into before.

Your DNA is not the same as Christ's DNA. When Jesus transferred His DNA to the blind man's eyes, He gave us a study in contrasts for what we cannot see now but will see through the eyes of our hearts by the power of His Spirit. If we want to see spiritually, then we must be willing to open our eyes by faith, even when there is mud from our past obscuring our vision. God's Word tells us, "Now faith is confidence in what we hope for and assurance about what we do not see" (Hebrews 11:1).

In other words, with your DNA you cannot see.

But with His DNA, you will see *His glory*.

With your DNA you are a victim.

With His DNA you are *more than a conqueror*.

With your DNA you are limited.

With His DNA you can do *all things* through Christ who gives you strength.

With your DNA you will make excuses.

But with His DNA, you will *make history*.

Perhaps your DNA stands for deoxyribonucleic acid, but His DNA stands for Divinity Now Accessible! More than two thousand years ago, Jesus walked this planet as a human being of flesh and blood. He died, was resurrected, ascended to heaven and transferred so much more than even the DNA in His spittle could have contained.

What Christ gave us was not His spit, but His Spirit!

Heavenly Power

When you think about gifts you have received, what are some of the best ones? Perhaps a large amount of cash at graduation or when you got married? A special piece of jewelry on a birthday or anniversary? Maybe even a car for Christmas, just like all the automakers try to depict in their holiday commercials? Whatever your best gifts have been, I promise that none can compare with the gift Jesus has given you.

Too often we tend to think about gifts as being tangible items and material possessions of special value. But the very best gifts usually exceed our expectations. They are the gifts that we did not realize we needed. Or that we did not realize are more powerful than we might assume.

Such is the case with the gift Jesus left His followers. While He had alluded to this gift before His death (see John 15:26), after His resurrection, Jesus let the disciples know that His gift's arrival was imminent:

> After his suffering, he presented himself to them and gave many convincing proofs that he was alive. He appeared to them over a period of forty days and spoke about the kingdom of God. On one occasion, while he was eating with them, he gave them this command: "Do not leave Jerusalem, but wait for the gift my Father promised, which you have heard me speak about. For John baptized with water, but in a few days you will be baptized with the Holy Spirit." Then they gathered around him and asked him, "Lord, are you at this time going to restore the kingdom to Israel?" He said to them: "It is not for you to know the times or dates the Father has set by his own authority. But you will receive power when the Holy Spirit comes on you; and you will be my witnesses in Jerusalem, and in all Judea and Samaria, and to the ends of the earth."
>
> Acts 1:3–8

Because Jesus knew the disciples were making plans for when He would no longer be with them, He commanded them to stay put until they received the gift of the Holy Spirit. Their response reveals a great deal about how we continue to react when we want to connect with God and have access to His power. The disciples circled around Jesus and asked if this would be when He restored the kingdom of Israel. They wanted to know dates and details of when Christ would overthrow the Romans and reestablish Israel's independence.

Even after all they had been through together, after all they had heard Jesus say and witnessed Him do, apparently the disciples, some of them at least, assumed Jesus was going to restore Israel through earthly methods. But Jesus made it clear that this was not their concern. "It is not for you to know the times or dates the Father has set by his own authority" (Acts 1:7). They should focus, instead, on the power they would receive through the Holy Spirit, which would allow them to share the Gospel throughout the known world at that time and to the ends of the earth.

Too often I wonder if we want dates, times and details from God when He wants to give us more of His Spirit and more of His power. We are focused on the "when," and He is focused on giving us the "how." We cannot see a way forward, so we want the Lord to spell it out for us. "I know You're going to help me get through this trial, Lord," we say, "but what is that going to look like and when will it end? Could You please give me the time and date?"

When you get hung up on the details of what God is doing in your life, you may miss out on the delivery. When you are focused only on how messy your process seems, you may miss out on the miracle of His promise. When you are blinded by the temporary obstacles of the present, you might miss out on the eternal perspective of your future.

If we think we need to understand how the miracle works before we receive it, then we are getting in the way of what God wants to give us. Our brain is a wonderful organ in our body. Our intellect is a gift that helps us reason, think, remember, analyze, create and choose. But our mind can get in the way of receiving God's Spirit if we let our rational, logical ways guard the gates of our hearts.

Just imagine if the man blind from birth had limited the miracle of his own healing by focusing on the method Jesus chose. "Lord, did You just spit on the ground? Uh, I know You are the Son of God and all, but that is kind of gross. Oh, and now You are rubbing Your saliva in the dirt to make some mud? That sounds really dirty and messy, so—hey, please do not come near me with Your muddy hands! Are You putting that over my eyes right now? Oooh, please don't do that! How can mud give me sight?"

IF WE THINK WE NEED TO UNDERSTAND HOW THE MIRACLE WORKS BEFORE WE RECEIVE IT, THEN WE ARE GETTING IN THE WAY OF WHAT GOD WANTS TO GIVE US.

We can laugh at the absurdity of such a nearsighted, forest-for-the-trees response, but how often do we basically resist the power God wants to give us because it feels too messy? How often are we missing opportunities to receive all the resources of the Holy Spirit because we do not think it feels the way we thought it would? We expect earthly details, and God gives us heavenly power.

We think we are waiting on God for whatever we have been asking to receive, and He is waiting on us to realize we already have access to it through the power of His Spirit.

Blowing in the Wind

When the gift of the Holy Spirit arrived, it was unmistakable. Because the disciples had been focused on details and dates at their conversation before the ascension, perhaps Christ wanted to make sure they realized this was it. For there was nothing subtle about its arrival or its impact.

> When the day of Pentecost came, they were all together in one place. Suddenly a sound like the blowing of a violent wind came from heaven and filled the whole house where they were sitting. They saw what seemed to be tongues of fire that separated and came to rest on each of them. All of them were filled with the Holy Spirit and began to speak in other tongues as the Spirit enabled them.
>
> Acts 2:1–4

As the followers of Jesus began to speak in spiritual tongues, they started to attract a crowd. The variety of languages that people heard being spoken drew them in. At first these onlookers assumed these Spirit-filled believers to be drunk on wine, but then Peter began to explain. He used the opportunity to preach the Gospel. The power and movement of this new Spirit speaking through Peter had an enormous impact for God's Kingdom. "Those who accepted his message were baptized, and about three thousand were added to their number that day" (Acts 2:41).

We have many other examples of the Holy Spirit at work in the early Church. And the power those followers of Jesus received is the same power we receive when we accept God's gift of salvation through Jesus and invite the Spirit to dwell in our hearts. The Bible promises, "The Spirit of God, who raised Jesus from the dead, lives in you. And just as God raised Christ Jesus from the dead, he will give life to your mortal bodies by this same Spirit living within you" (Romans 8:11 NLT).

My friend, you have the resurrection power of Jesus Christ dwelling in you. This is the same kind of death-conquering power God used to raise His Son from the dead. Through the power of the

Holy Spirit, there is nothing you cannot accomplish for God's glory. You simply have to allow the mud to fall away so that you can see clearly. You only must step out in faith and discover all that God has for you.

No matter how dirty, muddy or grimy you think your situation has become, if you have been washed in the blood of the Lamb, then you can be whiter than snow. You may have messed up, given in, fallen down, tripped over, stumbled in and stayed down more times than you can count. But you will always rise again by the resurrection power infusing every ounce of your being.

Unstoppable Spirit

When we receive the Holy Spirit, we experience a divine friendship unlike any other. Prior to His death and resurrection, Jesus told His followers, "I will ask the Father, and he will give you another Advocate, who will never leave you. He is the Holy Spirit, who leads into all truth" (John 14:16–17 NLT). The word rendered as *advocate* here is from the Greek *parakaleo*, or *paraclete*, which also means "counselor, friend, and helper."[3] In fact, the term literally refers to someone called alongside to help you carry something heavy, such as a log.

Once God's Spirit has come into our lives, we are never alone. He guides us, knows us, comforts us and reveals to us. He empowers us and enlightens us. He restores our sight when we are temporarily blinded by circumstances, emotions or temptations. The Holy Spirit does all these things and so much more. But allow me to clarify what He is *not*:

The Holy Spirit is not a denomination.
The Holy Spirit is not a network.

The Holy Spirit is not an emotion.

The Holy Spirit is not an experience.

The Holy Spirit is not a moment.

The Holy Spirit is not a service.

The Holy Spirit is not a conference.

The Holy Spirit is not an ideology.

The Holy Spirit is not a philosophy.

The Holy Spirit is not an app.

Simply put, the Holy Spirit is the most powerful person and force on planet earth today! This means that the most powerful spirit alive today is not the spirit of the cancel culture. It is not the spirit of socialism or communism, consumerism or capitalism. It is not the spirit of abortion or pedophilia. It is not the spirit of success and fame, social media or online influencers.

The unequivocal most powerful Spirit on our planet today is still the Holy Spirit of almighty God, the Comforter, the Advocate, the Paraclete!

We are assured by God's Word:

- "'Not by might nor by power, but by My Spirit,' says the LORD" (Zechariah 4:6 NKJV).
- "You will receive power when the Holy Spirit comes on you" (Acts 1:8).
- "Where the Spirit of the Lord is, there is freedom" (2 Corinthians 3:17).

Do you believe the Holy Spirit is working in your life right now at this very moment?

If you believe it, *praise* like you have that Spirit.

If you believe it, *pray* like you have that Spirit.

If you believe it, *prophesy* like you have that Spirit.

If you believe it, *live* like you have that Spirit.

"Do not quench the Spirit" (1 Thessalonians 5:19) by getting mired in the mud. Nothing can stop the power of the Holy Spirit when it is unleashed in your life. There is not an executive order, a Supreme Court decision, a legislative initiative, a universal law or a social media campaign that has the power to stop the Holy Spirit from moving upon the face of the earth. Not war, famine, disease, disaster or calamity. Not betrayal, bankruptcy or bitterness.

The White House cannot stop the Spirit.

Congress cannot stop the Spirit.

The courts cannot stop the Spirit.

Facebook cannot stop the Spirit.

Google cannot stop the Spirit.

TikTok cannot stop the Spirit.

No one can cancel, unplug, de-platform or defund the Holy Spirit.

This same Spirit dwells in you, my friend. You have the identical Spirit who raised Jesus from the dead living inside of you (see Romans 8:11). And you know what this means? If Jesus came out of the tomb, you can come out of anything.

With that Spirit you can come out of addiction.

With that Spirit you can come out of depression.

With that Spirit you can come out of anxiety.

With that Spirit you can come out of bondage.

With that Spirit you can come out of shame.

With that Spirit you can come out of the past.

It is time to open your eyes to the power of the Holy Spirit in your life!

—————— OPEN YOUR EYES ——————

Here are some questions to assist you in applying this chapter's eye-opening truths and Spirit-fueled motivators. Use this time of reflection and prayer as an opportunity to come before God and receive a fresh breath of the Holy Spirit's presence in your life. Remember, He is your Friend and Advocate, who is there alongside you in the midst of whatever you may be facing right now.

So take a few moments to calm your mind and quiet your heart in prayer before allowing the Spirit to guide and speak to you. Ask Him to reveal any areas of your life that are displeasing to God so that you can confess and repent. Seek His wisdom for those questions and problems over which you have been pondering and fretting. Allow His whisper to speak into your life so that you can feel God's presence and power in every moment of every day.

1. When have you experienced a season that seemed especially "muddy" that kept you mired in doubt, fear and uncertainty? How did God pull you out of the mud?

2. How have you prevented yourself from receiving all God wants to give you by focusing on earthly details instead of heavenly power? What can you do to allow Him full access to all areas of your life?

3. When have you most recently experienced the unmistakable presence and power of the Holy Spirit? How is He currently working in your life?

Dear God, I give You thanks and praise for the amazing gift of Your Spirit in my life. I am so grateful for the new life I have in You. Thank You for the comfort, counsel and courage You give me through the Spirit each day. Forgive me for the times I doubt You or allow circumstances and emotions to blind me to the Holy Spirit's presence. I know Your resurrection power is in my life, making me more than a conqueror for every obstacle, adversary and barrier I may encounter. Allow me to trust You more as I continue opening my eyes to walk by spiritual sight and not by my earthly senses. In Jesus' name, Amen.

Mud Pies

Open Your Eyes to God's Original Design

Through the resurrection power of Jesus, God reactivates His original plan for you.

You must give Him access to your dirt before He grants you access to your destiny.

A ll mud is not the same.

Its consistency relies on the ratio of dirt to liquid as well as other environmental factors, particularly temperature and rainfall. The quality and amount of ingredients—specifically phosphorous, potassium and nitrogen—make a big difference as well. I am not much of a gardener, and no one will ever mistake me for a farmer. I have never had the proverbial green thumb, but I do have a green eye—I know a healthy, beautiful plant when I see one.

Growing up in Pennsylvania, in Bethlehem near the Lehigh Valley, I quickly learned to appreciate my home state's agricultural legacy. As one of the original thirteen colonies, the Keystone State quickly became known for its rich, fertile soil, abundant rainfall and temperate climate. Settlers called Pennsylvania a "farmer's heaven" and even "America's breadbasket," and from the 1720s through the 1840s, it led the colonies and new states in food production. Wheat, flax, cotton, vegetables and livestock not only provided for local inhabitants but resulted in plentiful supply for exports to the West Indies and Europe.[1]

My state history lessons, significant as they were during my boyhood, cannot compare to the much more tangible way I learned to appreciate Pennsylvania's farming legacy—its delicious produce. Occasionally, especially on Saturday mornings in the summer, our family would go to a local farmers' market. A few of those times, we drove about ten miles to nearby Easton in order to visit the oldest continuous open-air market in the United States.[2]

The Easton Farmers' Market that was established in 1752 featured a variety of locally grown fresh fruits and vegetables. Some stalls would offer samples, and nothing beat the taste of a ripe strawberry or juicy peach. You could also find natural cheeses, fresh eggs, artisan meats and baked goods. Depending on the season, this historical market would be littered with bright sunflowers, daisies, hydrangeas and geraniums.

But late summer into early fall was my favorite time. Crisp, just-picked apples overflowed bushel baskets that were competing for space with dozens of enormous orange pumpkins. As I grew older and began to recognize the difference in taste between store-bought fruit and veggies and the produce from the farmers' market, I asked my parents what accounted for the distinction. And my father told me, "The difference is in the soil."

Divinity in Dust

That thought—about the difference being in the soil—came to mind recently when I was reflecting on the miracle of Jesus healing the man who had been blind since birth. Christ chose to make mud from His saliva and dirt from the ground where He stood. The mud pie He created was unlike any other. Certainly, for the blind man, the miracle in the mud made all the difference.

The mud mask placed over his sightless eyes not only contained divine DNA, but it also contained the dirt of his homeland. Jesus brought His supernatural healing power and used what was already there to produce this messy miracle. "Then he spit on the ground, made mud with the saliva, and spread the mud over the blind man's eyes" (John 9:6 NLT). Jesus infused the dusty ground of earth with the unlimited power of heaven.

This unique combination recalls the way God created man to begin with: "Then the LORD God formed a man from the dust of the ground and breathed into his nostrils the breath of life, and the man became a living being" (Genesis 2:7). Instead of saliva, God breathed the breath of life into the man He formed from the dust of the ground, whom He created in His own image (see Genesis 1:27). Just as Jesus did with the blind man, God the Father instilled life into dust to create something new.

The miraculous mud Jesus made also symbolizes who He was, both God and man, when living in this world. The Bible tells us that the Son of God was fully human while also fully, perfectly divine, which enabled Him to atone for our sins once and for all, paying the debt we could not pay.

> For this reason he had to be made like them, fully human in every way, in order that he might become a merciful and faithful high priest in service to God, and that he might make atonement for the sins of the people. Because he himself suffered when he was tempted, he is able to help those who are being tempted.
>
> Hebrews 2:17–18

By choosing to add His supernatural saliva to the dusty ground, Jesus illustrated how He bridges heaven and earth, enabling all of us not only to see spiritually but to experience relationship with God our Father. Consider how the gospel of John describes the incarnation of Christ. "The Word became flesh and made his dwelling among us. We have seen his glory, the glory of the one and only Son, who came from the Father, full of grace and truth" (John 1:14).

We have access to this same incarnational power when we invite the Holy Spirit to dwell in us. Sometimes, though, we do not follow through on obeying God's commands and instructions. Our faith remains weak and immature while our commitment to God stays half-hearted. We do not experience God's power and presence fully unleashed in our lives. We do not produce healthy spiritual fruit that fulfills our true potential.

Why? Because we do not provide fertile soil.

How Does Your Garden Grow?

Remember the old nursery rhyme that asked, "How does your garden grow?"[3] We might do well to ask ourselves this same question. On any given day, what do you rely on to get through your day? How often do you allow God's Spirit to empower and guide you? While you may want to trust God and walk by faith each day, many people do not experience it because they are not growing and maturing in their faith.

When we accept the free gift of salvation through Jesus Christ and welcome the indwelling of His Spirit, we experience what Jesus described as being "born again" (John 3:3), because just as our bodies were born from flesh, "the Spirit gives birth to spirit" (John 3:6). And what exactly does this mean? "This means that anyone who belongs to Christ has become a new person. The old life is gone; a new life has begun!" (2 Corinthians 5:17 NLT).

This new life we have comes from Christ through the power of His Spirit in us. Jesus told His followers:

> "I am the vine; you are the branches. If you remain in me and I in you, you will bear much fruit; apart from me you can do nothing. If you do not remain in me, you are like a branch that is thrown away and withers; such branches are picked up, thrown into the fire and burned. If you remain in me and my words remain in you, ask whatever you wish, and it will be done for you. This is to my Father's glory, that you bear much fruit, showing yourselves to be my disciples."
>
> John 15:5–8

In other words, we only experience true spiritual growth by remaining in Christ's power and obeying His commands. Notice that when we go our own way and choose not to remain in Christ, then we wither and die. When His words take root in our hearts, however, we have full access to the limitless, infinite power of almighty God!

Which brings us back to the kind of soil we provide. How we cultivate, fertilize, nurture, protect and grow the power of the living Word in ourselves makes all the difference. In a revealing exploration of how we live in Him, Jesus told a parable that illustrates the various ways people tend to respond to His presence in their lives:

WHEN HIS WORDS TAKE ROOT IN OUR HEARTS, WE HAVE FULL ACCESS TO THE LIMITLESS, INFINITE POWER OF ALMIGHTY GOD!

> "Listen! A farmer went out to sow his seed. As he was scattering the seed, some fell along the path, and the birds came and ate it up.

Some fell on rocky places, where it did not have much soil. It sprang up quickly, because the soil was shallow. But when the sun came up, the plants were scorched, and they withered because they had no root. Other seed fell among thorns, which grew up and choked the plants, so that they did not bear grain. Still other seed fell on good soil. It came up, grew and produced a crop, some multiplying thirty, some sixty, some a hundred times." Then Jesus said, "Whoever has ears to hear, let them hear."

Mark 4:3–9

In the culture of that time, natural examples and agricultural illustrations likely provided the broadest access for the most people. One did not need to be a farmer to understand the items Jesus used to convey His message—vines and branches, seeds and soils, birds and thorns. These everyday symbols were prevalent and plentiful and made lessons of spiritual truth concrete and tangible.

Nonetheless, notice how Christ concluded—"if you have ears to hear, then listen." In other words, He was not speaking in code or in a complicated literary style. He was not using parables in His teaching to disguise or obscure the truth. He was doing just the opposite. The irony, though, is that despite Him making this lesson easier to grasp and apply by telling a parable, some people, including His own disciples, still did not get it.

The Purpose of Parables

Have you ever heard a speaker speak or a teacher teach but had no clue what they were talking about? Sometimes there is a language barrier, which is why I like to use both English and Spanish when I preach. If someone does not get my message in one language, I trust the Spirit to help them understand it in the other.

But there are also times when the language is clear and the words are familiar, yet you still cannot put them together cohesively. You have a hard time following along with where the speaker or teacher wants to take you. The vocabulary seems too elevated or even pretentious, the syntax too complex and lengthy. The examples and illustrations might seem unrelatable, depending on the person's background, ethnicity and social culture. Sometimes the ideas and concepts may simply be too abstract and intellectual for most listeners to grasp.

None of these issues was apparently the problem with those who were listening to Jesus' parable that day, and yet they still struggled with fully comprehending what their Master wanted to convey.

When he was alone, the Twelve and the others around him asked him about the parables. He told them, "The secret of the kingdom of God has been given to you. But to those on the outside everything is said in parables so that, 'they may be ever seeing but never perceiving, and ever hearing but never understanding; otherwise they might turn and be forgiven!'"

Mark 4:10–12

Before Jesus explained the meaning behind the parable of the sower, He addressed the larger issue of why He used parables in the first place. On one hand, as I just mentioned, they made spiritual concepts easier to grasp by illustrating them with concrete scenarios that would be familiar to most people. But on the other hand, the use of parables served as a kind of filter for the truth of who Christ is and His message of grace.

Hearing the message in Christ's parable required more than auditory functionality; it required a tender, open heart and a sincere desire to understand. The people listening heard His words with their ears but heard and received His message with their hearts. In other words, you have to at least be willing to believe in order for the Word to take root inside you.

But for "those on the outside," presumably the Jewish religious leaders and Pharisees, the parables would not speak to them because their hearts were hard and calloused. Most of them apparently felt threatened and intimidated by Christ's claims, and they refused to recognize Him as the long-promised Messiah. They, in fact, wanted to trap or trick Him into violating the law—either the Jewish Law of Moses or the law of the Roman government, or both. This is the tactic we saw them employ in the previous chapter, when they brought the woman who had been caught in adultery before Jesus.

They were not listening with their hearts, only their ears.

Soil Samples

To emphasize His point about the purpose of parables, Jesus alluded to verses from the prophet Isaiah (see 6:9–10), quoting the message that God gave to Isaiah to relay to the rebellious people of Israel at that time. These verses focus on the defensive posture of those who were unwilling to seek God. They see but never perceive, hear but never understand. Basically, Jesus compares those attacking and criticizing Him to the hard-hearted people of Israel in generations past. The implication is that those on the outside who do not understand the parable are rebellious, proud and far from God. But just to avoid any misunderstanding, Jesus went on to answer His disciples' question about the meaning of the parable directly:

> Then Jesus said to them, "Don't you understand this parable? How then will you understand any parable? The farmer sows the word.

Some people are like seed along the path, where the word is sown. As soon as they hear it, Satan comes and takes away the word that was sown in them. Others, like seed sown on rocky places, hear the word and at once receive it with joy. But since they have no root, they last only a short time. When trouble or persecution comes because of the word, they quickly fall away. Still others, like seed sown among thorns, hear the word; but the worries of this life, the deceitfulness of wealth and the desires for other things come in and choke the word, making it unfruitful. Others, like seed sown on good soil, hear the word, accept it, and produce a crop—some thirty, some sixty, some a hundred times what was sown."

Mark 4:13–20

I love the fact that Jesus refused to leave His followers uncertain about His message with this parable. Like a literature teacher explaining a short story to eager students, Christ spells out what each item in the story means. Farmers, those who speak the truth of the Gospel, sow the Word, which you will recall is another name for Jesus (see John 1:1–16), to those who hear them preach and teach. Whether or not the Word takes root so that they grow spiritually depends on the quality of the soil and how each person responds to adverse conditions.

Some people are like shallow soil along the path; they are robbed by the enemy before the seed can take root. Apparently, they hear the Word but do not know how to cultivate it in the midst of assaults from the devil. They have no spiritual armor or connection to God's power to win these battles.

Next comes rocky soil. These people receive the Word with joy but do not allow it to sink into a deeper level where it can take root—apparently because they do not have a deeper level. Trials, adversity and persecution kill the seed in them because the Word is not rooted deeply enough. Perhaps they are unwilling to trust God beyond their circumstances.

Thorny ground proves just as hazardous. These people hear the Word, but then deceit, worry and greed for the things of the world choke out the seed and prevent it from growing. They have too many other consuming demands in their life that do not leave room for the Word to grow.

Finally, the good soil provides the fertile environment where the Word can take root in the lives of those who hear it. Their seed grows and produces an abundant crop. While it may vary in quantity, their soil has produced healthy, plentiful fruit. This soil illustrates what happens when we cultivate and nurture the Word—we produce the fruit of the Spirit.

Surrender Your Soil

So how do we cultivate good soil in our lives so that we grow in the Spirit and produce good fruit? By infusing our dirt with the divine! Just as Jesus spit to make mud for the blind man's miracle, we must live in the fullness of the Holy Spirit and pour His power into the ground of our lives. He has the power to make miracles in the mess of the mundane. But you must give God access to your dirt before He grants you access to your destiny.

YOU MUST GIVE GOD ACCESS TO YOUR DIRT BEFORE HE GRANTS YOU ACCESS TO YOUR DESTINY.

I mean this both literally and figuratively. When you surrender your life to Christ, you allow His Spirit to dwell in your heart and plant the seed of truth. The way you keep the soil of your heart fertile is by weeding out all the worldly things that try to crowd your life.

Therefore, rid yourselves of all malice and all deceit, hypocrisy, envy, and slander of every kind. Like newborn babies, crave pure spiritual milk, so that by it you may grow up in your salvation, now that you have tasted that the Lord is good.

1 Peter 2:1–3

Almost anything that grows also needs light, including your spirit as you walk by faith in God's light. "For you were once darkness, but now you are light in the Lord. Live as children of light" (Ephesians 5:8). Once you begin growing and maturing in your faith, then you begin to glimpse the new life God has for you. Your new life in Christ allows God to fulfill all He has created you to be. When you live without the power of the Spirit, you diverge from God's plan for your life. When you live in the power of the Spirit, you experience God's best for your life.

In God's Word, He tells us, "Before I formed you in the womb I knew you, before you were born I set you apart" (Jeremiah 1:5). Similarly, we see the psalmist acknowledge that "you made all the delicate, inner parts of my body and knit me together in my mother's womb" (Psalm 139:13 NLT). No matter what has happened in your life, God can use that soil—even the rocky, thorny, shallow soil of your past—to grow you beyond anything you can imagine. "'For I know the plans I have for you,' says the LORD. 'They are plans for good and not for disaster, to give you a future and a hope'" (Jeremiah 29:11 NLT).

You are no accident, my friend. You are the son or daughter of the King of kings. You are joint heirs with Christ. You were born according to the model of the second Adam. And who is the second Adam? Jesus Christ, God's only Son, who came to earth and lived as a man in order to forgive your sins, wash you clean and empower you to live the life God designed you to live. Paul explains this transformation from the old to the new in his letter to the believers at Corinth:

> So it is written: "The first man Adam became a living being"; the last Adam, a life-giving spirit. The spiritual did not come first, but the natural, and after that the spiritual. The first man was of the dust of the earth; the second man is of heaven. As was the earthly man, so are those who are of the earth; and as is the heavenly man, so also are those who are of heaven. And just as we have borne the image of the earthly man, so shall we bear the image of the heavenly man.
>
> 1 Corinthians 15:45–49

When you surrender your soil to God's Spirit, God transforms you into the likeness of His perfect, holy Son. Right now, no matter what you may be facing, God is going to the beginning. God is returning to the original architectural design of humanity in order to align the original with the *now*. Where you are in your life and in your faith is where God meets you—*right now, right here!* Because Jesus came to save you, deliver you, heal you and reactivate His original plan for you.

Yes, God has a plan for you.

God has a plan for your children.

God has a plan for your children's children.

God has a plan for your now and for your next.

In God's original plan, you are not blind.

In God's original plan, you are not an addict.

In God's original plan, you are not an alcoholic.

In God's original plan, you are not broken.

In God's original plan, you are not full of anxiety.

In God's original plan, you are not the tail.

In God's original plan, you are not cursed.

In God's original plan, there is no such thing as a black church, a white church or any other color. There are only God's people in the church, the body of Christ.

In God's original plan, you are blessed.

You are not where you were.

You are not how you were.

You are not what others did to you.

You are not what you did to yourself.

You are who God says you are.

You are what God says you are.

You are an overcomer!

Power to Overcome

Christ followers have no other choice but to overcome. When the Holy Spirit is allowed to grow into all areas of your life, you flourish and thrive as never before. You overcome all that has held you back. To overcome is to defeat, to conquer, to triumph over and to win.

You can overcome what other people did to you. What other people have said about you. What you have falsely believed about yourself. What the world says about you. What the world does to you. Jesus said, "I have told you these things, so that in me you may have peace. In this world you will have trouble. But take heart! I have overcome the world" (John 16:33). Through the power of Christ in you, you cannot help but overcome anything that prevents you from being all God made you to be. You are more than a conqueror (see Romans 8:37)—you are an *overcomer*.

The enemy of your soul, the devil, wants you to nod in agreement right now without letting this truth take root deep in the soil of your soul. He wants you to agree in theory but not in practice. He wants to crowd the garden of your spirit with so many temptations, trials and tribulations that you turn away from tending to the growth of God's Spirit in you. But you must not let him.

The enemy has no authority over you, which is why he spends his time lying to you, deceiving you and tempting you. He cannot kill the seed of the Spirit growing inside you. Why? Because Christ defeated the power of death through the resurrection power of the Spirit—the same Spirit that dwells in you.

When the devil tries to lie to you, accuse you and tempt you, when he comes to steal your joy and rob your peace, you must stand firm in your faith through the power of the Spirit. God's Word makes it abundantly clear that you have all you need as an overcomer to vanquish your enemy and thrive in the Spirit. Christ's victory has secured your power to overcome the accuser:

"Now have come the salvation and the power and the kingdom of our God, and the authority of his Messiah. For the accuser of our brothers and sisters, who accuses them before our God day and night, has been hurled down. They triumphed over him by the blood of the Lamb and by the word of their testimony; they did not love their lives so much as to shrink from death. Therefore rejoice, you heavens and you who dwell in them! But woe to the earth and the sea, because the devil has gone down to you! He is filled with fury, because he knows that his time is short."

Revelation 12:10–12

God's power has always enabled His people to overcome. We see it repeatedly throughout the Bible. This book is not the book of perfect people. This sacred text is not a historical categorization of pristine, unblemished or stainless saints. Without a doubt, from Genesis to Revelation, this is a book of overcomers.

Abraham overcame the lies—including his own.

Joseph overcame the pit and the betrayal of his brothers.

Moses overcame his past, his temper and Pharaoh.

Joshua overcame the disobedience of his troops, and when his mentor died, his fear of being alone.

Gideon overcame the threshing floor.

Samson overcame his pride, his lack of respect for the anointing and Delilah's deception.

David overcame Saul's spear, a bear, a lion, a giant and his own moral turpitude.

Esther overcame the haters.

Daniel overcame the lions.

The Hebrew boys overcame the furnace.

Job overcame the loss of everything.

Peter overcame the cursing of his blessing.

Paul overcame the shipwreck and the snake.

And Jesus, the Son of God, incarnate on earth to do for us what we could not do for ourselves, overcame darkness, death and defeat. Jesus overcame everything!

So now it is time to add your name to this list. Think for a moment about what you believe is holding you back in your faith—your past mistakes, your weaknesses, your wounds from others, everything and anything that you believe impedes your spiritual growth and the work of God's Spirit in your life. No matter what you might believe holds you back, I am here to tell you the following undeniable truth: *You are—in Christ, by Christ and for Christ—an overcomer.*

And just so we are clear, let me tell you what you are not. You are not an eternal victim. You are not the devil's punching bag. You are not cursed. You are not defeated.

JESUS OVERCAME EVERYTHING! Everyone has overcome something. You would not be reading this right now if you had not overcome pain, sorrow, anger, fear, depression, anxiety or doubt. It may still creep in from time to time, like a weed trying to displace the blossom of faith in your life, but overcomers know how to get rid of weeds.

Just consider for a moment all the things in your life that you have overcome, especially those things that felt unbearable, unimaginable or intolerable at the time. Abuse, grief, trauma, poverty, bankruptcy, divorce and shame—they felt as if they would destroy you. But they did not. You persevered, you trusted and you overcame. What did you overcome to be where you are right now?

You overcame generational strongholds.

You overcame failure.

You overcame defeat.

You overcame sin.

You overcame temptation.

You overcame addiction.

You overcame depression.

You overcame anxiety.

You overcame confusion.

You overcame infirmity.

You overcame betrayal.

You overcame brokenness.

You overcame unbelief.

You overcame unforgiveness.

You overcame negativity.

You overcame toxic relationships.

You overcame the devil.

You overcame others.

And above all, you overcame yourself!

But *how?*

How did you overcome?

How did you make it?

How did you come out of that season?

How did you overcome the obstacles?

How did you overcome the haters?

How did you overcome everything hell sent your way?

Not with your personality, not with your social media postings, not with your tweets, not with your selfies, not with your political affiliation, not with your biology and not with your ideology.

You overcame by the blood of the Lamb and the word of your testimony! Whether you overcame thirty years ago or thirty days ago or thirty minutes ago, you called on the name of the Lord and experienced the power of His Spirit in you. Do not let anything choke your growth as you mature in your faith. God has breathed new life into you through the Spirit. Jesus has entered into the muddy mess of your mistakes and missteps and washed you clean in His blood.

Open your eyes and see the new life inside you!

——— OPEN YOUR EYES ———

You know how this works by now. Use the questions below to help you think through the powerful points in this chapter and how they apply to your life. Allow this time of reflection and prayer to be an opportunity to experience greater intimacy with God and rely on more of the Holy Spirit's power in your life. Do not forget—no matter what you may be facing, you are an overcomer.

Quiet your heart before God and allow His Spirit to comfort you and speak into your life. Think about your spiritual growth rate and what weeds might need pulling so that you can focus more deliberately on praying, studying the Bible and serving others with your God-given gifts. Ask the Spirit to show you rocky areas in your spiritual soil that need tilling so that you can produce greater fruit. Bask in the light of Christ so that you can thrive.

1. How would you describe your spiritual soil right now in your current season of life? What is the basis for this description?
2. What weeds keep springing up in your life to thwart your growth and slow down your spiritual progress? What can you do to weed out those things that distract you and divert your attention from God?

3. What are some of the greatest obstacles in your life that you have overcome through God's power? How did you see Him work in you and through you to empower you so that you could persevere and overcome them?

Dear Lord, I know there are areas of my life that I need to surrender to You. Forgive me for yielding to temptation and anything I have done to grieve Your Spirit dwelling inside me. Thank You for Your mercy and lovingkindness, which washes me clean and waters the soil of my spirit. Show me what to take away and what to add in my life so that I can be all that You created me to be. Prune any branches in my life that are displeasing to You and not bearing fruit. I know that You will continue to nourish my faith so that I can experience even more of Your miraculous power in the dusty, dirty mess of this world. In Jesus' name, Amen.

Double Blind

Open Your Eyes to a Holy Mess

Circumstances may blindside you, but you do not have to remain in the dark.

If you want to see clearly, you must be willing to worship while wounded.

I have been told that sometimes I sound more like a schoolteacher than a church pastor.

I never take offense at this and, in fact, consider it a compliment. Education has always been a passionate priority for me. When I was in college, I considered being a teacher and possibly even starting my own charter school. After I graduated, I taught government classes, civics classes and some honors courses at the high school in my hometown of Bethlehem, Pennsylvania.

As much as I enjoyed teaching, that vertical calling was soon overpowered by a horizontal calling as God led me into a broader ministry to serve all people, not just students. But my passion for education and its vital importance for Latino youth has never diminished. Anyone who knows me also knows that I am still a bit of the math nerd that I was growing up. I have never forgotten what I learned during the two years I studied computer engineering at Penn State before changing schools and majors.

One of the reasons I value education so much is its application to gain not simply knowledge but wisdom. Many of the foundational principles I learned as a young student have also served me well as life lessons. The scientific method, for example, is something most of us learned in primary school. While it may seem obvious or even simplistic to citizens of the 21st century, the scientific method basically standardized the way we conduct most experiments.

Two great historical minds, Francis Bacon and Isaac Newton, are usually credited with defining the scientific method as formulation of a *hypothesis*, execution of an *experiment* that tests that hypothesis and recording *results* that either support, refute or reveal the need to revise the hypothesis. Sounds like common sense, but until Bacon and Newton ignited the scientific revolution in the seventeenth century, no one had defined the beginning, middle and end points for new and existing discoveries.[1]

Before you say, "Spare me the history lesson, Pastor Sam," allow me to point out that the scientific method remains alive and well today in virtually every field and academic discipline. Fundamentally, it remains the basis for discovering new medical treatments, vaccines and pharmaceutical medications. Research scientists, engineers, doctors and tech programmers use the scientific method as the preliminary structure for discovery and advancement. I can safely venture that your life has benefited in myriad ways because the scientific method was

THE WAY YOU INTERPRET YOUR LIFE'S TRIAL-AND-ERROR EVENTS MAY BE BLINDING YOU.

employed by inventors, innovators and entrepreneurs in addition to those users already mentioned.

Why should you care about the scientific method? Because you may be unintentionally living it out to your detriment. The way you interpret your life's trial-and-error events may be blinding you.

Subjective Bias

You see, the story you tell yourself about your identity, your purpose and your relationships—including how you view God—develops in large part by how you draw conclusions based on your life experiences. Simply put, most of us develop false beliefs based on inaccurate assumptions, others' opinions, subjective bias and traumatic experiences that distort the truth of who God says we are, how He wants us to live and the purpose He created us to fulfill.

Sometimes we glimpse the dissonance between the messages we tell ourselves and the objective evidence outside ourselves. Many people, for instance, often fixate on seeing themselves and their body image based on negative criticism and shaming from others. At an early age they were told that they were fat or thin, unattractive or stupid, untalented or unlovable. The messages might or might not have been direct and overt. Words, attitudes and events—from parents, siblings, friends, peers and media—communicate comprehensively.

But the debilitating impact is usually the same because we internalize those negative messages into a hypothesis. We assume that we must be who and what others say we are, and then we interpret our perceptions of ourselves, others and everything around us through these false beliefs. We do not see clearly; instead, we see through a set of false beliefs that become self-reinforcing and sometimes self-fulfilling.

Those painful, shaming messages that we carry poison our perspective. Despite how healthy and physically fit someone can be as an adult, for example, she can still consider herself too thin or too heavy based on the messages she perceived from her family, peers and culture. When she sees herself in a photo or mirror, the image staring back at her reflects the painful emotions of what others have told her rather than the accurate vision of present reality.

Body image is not the only emotional and psychological area that is affected by our false beliefs. Many people often have highly critical and perfectionistic criteria for their appearance, intelligence, work performance, achievements, relational happiness, parenting and financial earning power—or whatever aspect was emphasized and valued as their self-worth was defined. Their views of themselves are flawed by the conclusions they have formed from past events, conversations and relationships.

In psychology, *subjective bias* is the term used to describe the way participants in a study or experiment behave in ways to meet the expectations of those conducting the research. Essentially, it is a way of conforming and trying to perform well and get validation by giving those in charge what you think they want.[2]

This same tendency operates on some level when you filter your way of seeing with those past messages you have internalized into beliefs. Instead of getting validation from researchers, though, you validate the false beliefs that are holding you prisoner, no matter how critical, inaccurate and unhealthy they may be. Simply put, your subjective bias prevents you from seeing the truth of God's perspective.

How have you experienced this kind of self-critical bias? What false beliefs do you struggle to shake? What negative assumptions and past experiences tend to blindside you when your circumstances do not turn out as expected?

Perhaps you did not get the promotion you wanted so you tell yourself that you are not surprised because you know you are not talented enough (or smart enough or whatever enough). You reinforce this false belief, which likely will make it more challenging for you to risk applying for a promotion in the future.

This kind of self-sabotaging trap might emerge in your relationships. You find yourself drawn to the same kind of person who inevitably deceives and hurts you. Instead of realizing the cycle, however, you tell yourself that you must not deserve a healthy relationship.

This kind of sabotage might show up in your finances and how you handle debt. You falsely believe you are never going to have enough money and that you are always going to be in debt, so you do not follow a budget or monitor your spending habits.

No matter what issue is affected, until you face the truth about your false beliefs, you are blinding yourself to what God wants to do in you and through you.

Blame Game

The blind man Jesus healed likely harbored some false beliefs about himself. Because the Braille language had not been invented yet, this man who had been blind since birth could not read and remained uneducated. His inability to read and lack of education might have led the people around him to assume he was not intelligent. Because the blind man could not work in conventional trades of the day, people might have assumed he was untalented, unskilled and untrainable. This assumption likely contributed to the blind man believing he had no choice but to beg in order to survive.

Based on how the man behaved after Jesus gave him the gift of sight, I suspect this man was actually quite intelligent and a quick learner. In fact, based on how he handled being interrogated by the Jewish religious leaders, I believe he would have made an excellent attorney. He ended up sparring verbally with them twice.

You will recall that the people who knew him as the blind beggar, identified as his neighbors and acquaintances, at first doubted it was the same man (see John 9:8–9). When the man assured them that he was indeed the person who had been blind since birth, they remained inquisitive. Some were likely skeptical. They wanted to know how the man regained his sight, and then when he told them, they wanted to know where Jesus was.

Since the man did not know, this group of inquisitors took him before the Pharisees:

> They brought to the Pharisees the man who had been blind. Now the day on which Jesus had made the mud and opened the man's eyes was a Sabbath. Therefore the Pharisees also asked him how he had received his sight. "He put mud on my eyes," the man replied, "and I washed, and now I see." Some of the Pharisees said, "This man is not from God, for he does not keep the Sabbath." But others asked, "How can a sinner perform such signs?" So they were divided. Then they turned again to the blind man, "What have you to say about him? It was your eyes he opened." The man replied, "He is a prophet."
>
> John 9:13–17

Notice, not surprisingly, that the Pharisees focused *not* on the incredible miracle of the blind man receiving sight but on the fact that Jesus had healed him on the Sabbath, a religious day of rest with very strict rules regarding what one could and could not do under the Law of Moses. In fact, this was not the only instance when the Jewish religious leaders condemned Jesus and His disciples for doing something contrary to the law on a Sabbath.

The gospel of Mark tells of how Jesus and His disciples were walking along on a Sabbath when they started picking heads of grain to eat from the fields beside them. When the Pharisees condemned their actions as unlawful, Jesus countered by pointing to the example of David, who when hungry broke the law by eating consecrated bread from the house of God that was reserved only for priests (see Mark 2:23–26). Jesus concluded by emphasizing, "The Sabbath was made for man, not man for the Sabbath. So the Son of Man is Lord even of the Sabbath" (verses 27–28).

Because the Pharisees remained uncertain about what to do with Jesus' action of healing the blind man on a Sabbath, they doubted the miracle entirely and called for the man's parents so they could interrogate them (see John 9:18–19). Talk about subjective bias and circular reasoning! The Pharisees were so intent on denying that Jesus was the Messiah that they looked for other ways to discredit the muddy miracle rather than entertain the evidence before them. They refused to see the sighted man who was right in front of them.

You may experience the same reactions with certain people in your life. As the Lord produces a miracle from your mess, these individuals will look for explanations, excuses and indictments, but they will often refuse to acknowledge the unlimited power of God's Spirit that was unleashed in your life. They may work hard to remain skeptical, uncertain and disbelieving despite your testimony, in word and in deed, to the miraculous power of Jesus in your blind spots.

The man's parents, however, refused to fall into the religious leaders' blame game. They confirmed what was true. Yes, he was their son, and yes, he had been born blind. But they did not know who had healed him or how. Just to make it clear that they knew what the Pharisees were up to, the parents said, "Ask him. He is of age;

he will speak for himself" (John 9:21). So the Pharisees sent for the blind man to testify before them once again.

For God's Glory

While the miraculously sighted man's parents deftly sidestepped the trap of the Pharisees, they also put their son back on the hot seat. They stressed that their son was an adult, not a child. They could not speak for him even if they wanted to do so. The relentless, determined religious leaders brought the man back for a second round of grilling:

> A second time they summoned the man who had been blind. "Give glory to God by telling the truth," they said. "We know this man is a sinner." He replied, "Whether he is a sinner or not, I don't know. One thing I do know. I was blind but now I see!" Then they asked him, "What did he do to you? How did he open your eyes?" He answered, "I have told you already and you did not listen. Why do you want to hear it again? Do you want to become his disciples too?" Then they hurled insults at him and said, "You are this fellow's disciple! We are disciples of Moses! We know that God spoke to Moses, but as for this fellow, we don't even know where he comes from."
>
> John 9:24–29

Right off the bat, notice the irony of how they begin. "Give glory to God by telling the truth." The irony emerges at two levels here. First, the man had already told them the truth, but it was not the truth they wanted to hear. So now they added some pressure to glorify God by telling them their desired false truth.

Second, you will recall that when Jesus and His disciples first came upon the blind man, the disciples wanted to know if his blindness resulted from his sin or that of his parents. Jesus replied, "Neither . . . this happened so that the works of God might be displayed in him" (John 9:3). Basically, this man who had been blind but experienced the muddy, messy miracle at the hands of Jesus was a living testimony to God's glory already.

And are you hearing the implications for you and me of what Jesus said? This man, blind since birth, was not being punished for his sin or the sin of his parents. His blindness existed as an opportunity for God's power to be displayed. So often we wonder if certain painful events and traumatic losses are our own fault because of sinful choices we have made. While our sinful choices certainly carry consequences that are often painful, they present the same opportunity that this man's blindness presented—to showcase God's glory.

ARE YOU HEARING THE IMPLICATIONS FOR YOU AND ME OF WHAT JESUS SAID?

The Pharisees did not want to face the glory of God right in front of them. They wanted to hear this man parrot the falsehood they believed about the healer. "We know this man is a sinner." But the man looking at them refused to be manipulated. The recipient of new sight not only refused, but he stood up to these religious elitists.

Expert Testimony

In essence, the formerly blind man told the Pharisees, "Look, I've told you already and you didn't listen. Why do you want to hear it again? Why are you so obsessed with who healed me? Do you want to become His followers?" This man, clearly in a dangerous situation with the religious establishment of the day, saw their insistence for what it was. They were determined to find a way to discredit Christ by threat and intimidation. So when this man stood up to them, they naturally turned and began hurling insults at him.

Then comes my favorite part of this exchange, and the reason I believe he would have made an excellent attorney. The newly healed man laid out the facts in a way that was logical, reasonable and conclusive:

> The man answered, "Now that is remarkable! You don't know where he comes from, yet he opened my eyes. We know that God does not listen to sinners. He listens to the godly person who does his will. Nobody has ever heard of opening the eyes of a man born blind. If this man were not from God, he could do nothing." To this they replied, "You were steeped in sin at birth; how dare you lecture us!" And they threw him out.
>
> John 9:30–34

Notice the progressive sequence here. First, the man points out the hole in their attack. It is basically irrelevant where the healer came from. Knowing where Jesus was from—Nazareth, of course— still would not have explained why or how He was able to heal this man who had been blind since birth.

Then the man explained another line of reasoning. "Okay, we know God doesn't listen to sinners," he said, finding common ground with the Pharisees. "He listens to the godly person who does His will." In other words, if Jesus were a sinner—presumably of violating Sabbath law, as they claimed—then why would God work through Him?

The man then delivered the perfect closer: "Who has ever heard of anyone giving sight to a man born blind? Only someone from God could do it! Otherwise, it wouldn't have worked." Without a rational rebuttal, the Pharisees resorted once again to attempting to discredit the man before them. "How dare you! You were conceived in sin—you have no authority to lecture us regardless of how clearly right you may be."

Despite the fact that this man had testified to the miracle that he himself had experienced, despite the testimony of this man's parents, despite the second interrogation and this man's brilliant defense, the religious leaders closed their eyes even tighter. Rather than celebrate the miracle before them, rather than praise and worship God, rather than attempt to open their minds and hearts to the possibility that Jesus was the long-promised Messiah, the Pharisees chose blindness. They had no choice but to throw the man out.

Because in their hearts the fear that he was right must have overwhelmed them.

Shade and Shadows

If this man's story as told to us had ended when he went to the Pool of Siloam and came home seeing, or even after his neighbors and witnesses questioned him, then we might assume he more or less lived happily ever after (see John 9:7–12). But clearly that is not what happened. Suddenly, this man's messy miracle became even messier as he realized he was in the crosshairs of his healer's enemies.

We will explore the rest of this man's story in our remaining chapters, but I want to pause here for a moment and linger in the tension. Sometimes even when you get your miracle, what follows radically departs from your expectations. You assume that once you can see clearly that everything should be beautifully vivid and colorful; however, you then open your eyes to a world of shade and shadows.

Perhaps you thought after your miraculous recovery from cancer you would do nothing but rejoice—and then the medical bills come in and the debt collectors start calling. You expected that once your marriage had been healed by the power of God's Spirit that your spouse would love you exactly as you want to be loved—only to discover that old habits still linger. It might be that you finally got out of debt through an unexpected windfall from heaven—only to be grounded by the expense of replacing the roof on your house.

Just as the Pharisees could not stand to give Jesus credit for the blind man's miracle of sight, the enemy will look for opportunities to drag your miracle back into the mud. The devil will try to trigger old scripts and old responses that make you doubt your miracle and question the extent of God's power. The painful labels and stinging criticism of past haters will resurface as the enemy employs every method at his disposal to cloud your spiritual vision.

When this happens, you must keep your eyes open to the holy mess before you. Even if it is not what you expected—*especially* when it is not what you expected—you must trust God to meet you when you are still hurting after the miracle. That is when you embrace the tension of worshiping while wounded.

Worship While Wounded

When I think about messy miracles, another, perhaps even more dramatic, miracle comes to mind. This one appears much more personal for Christ because it involved not just one person He cared about, but a family of three siblings. "Jesus loved Martha, Mary, and Lazarus" (John 11:5 NLT). When their brother became seriously ill, the sisters sent word to Jesus, presumably in hopes that He would come right away and heal Lazarus (see John 11:3). But despite His great love for these friends, Jesus remained away for at least two more days before finally venturing to Bethany, where they lived.

When He arrived there, it appeared to be too late. "Lazarus had already been in his grave for four days" (John 11:17 NLT). Understandably, the two sisters were a bit confused as to why their friend, to whom they had sent word days earlier, had not arrived in time to save their brother. In the midst of their devastating messiness, however, Jesus performed a miracle that they did not anticipate:

> When Martha got word that Jesus was coming, she went to meet him. But Mary stayed in the house. . . . Jesus told her, "I am the resurrection and the life. Anyone who believes in me will live, even after dying. Everyone who lives in me and believes in me will never ever die. Do you believe this, Martha?" "Yes, Lord," she told him. "I have always believed you are the Messiah, the Son of God, the one who has come into the world from God." Then she returned to Mary. She called Mary aside from the mourners and told her, "The Teacher is here and wants to see you." So Mary immediately went to him. . . . Jesus responded, "Didn't I tell you that you would see God's glory if you believe?"
>
> John 11:20, 25–29, 40 NLT

Martha had to have been emotionally wounded, wrapped in her own shroud of grief and, most likely, deep disappointment. Martha surely carried pain—the pain of grief, of suffering, of brokenness. Yet the moment she heard that Jesus was near, she left the other mourners and rushed to meet Him. I do not know about you, but if I were in Martha's place, I am not one hundred percent sure I would run to see Him after my beloved family member had just died. I would like to believe my faith is that strong, but in the absolute messiest moments of life, it is hard to hope for the holy.

But Martha knew how to do something that all of us must learn to do in order to open our eyes and grow in our faith. She entered courageously into the terrible tension of acknowledging God's power and goodness in the midst of her own pain and sorrow. Martha knew that the presence of Jesus changes everything.

She had hard questions that only Jesus could answer. Her dear brother, and Jesus' beloved friend, had died. The only One who could have healed Lazarus did not show up on time. Now it was too late.

So what did Martha do? Instead of raging in anguish, instead of denouncing her faith and turning away from the One who had disappointed her, instead of going on social media or texting her disappointment, Martha ran toward the presence of Jesus.

She was wounded, but she ran. She was in pain, but she ran. And when she encountered Jesus, she not only shared her pain, but *she gave Him praise.* She not only vented, but she worshiped.

Martha cried out, "If You would have been there . . . because I know who You are. You are the Messiah. You are the Son of God." In other words, even though I am broken and hurting, I still know who You are. Even though I am shattered, I still know who You are. Even though I am devastated, I still know who You are. Even though I have never been more disappointed, I still know who You are. *And who You are is worthy of all my praise.*

Notice what Martha did not say. She did not say, "I thought You were the Messiah." She did not say, "I used to believe that You were the Son of God until You let my brother die." She did not speak in the past tense. She spoke in the present.

SHE NOT ONLY SHARED HER PAIN, BUT SHE GAVE HIM PRAISE.

"I know who You are! You are the Messiah! You are the Son of God!"

Martha dared to worship in the midst of her wounding.

Praise in the Pain

Opening your eyes to a holy mess requires that you worship the holy while grieving the mess. That is the essence of faith right there, my friend. The people who will change the world are born-again believers who are following Jesus Christ. They are disciples of the risen Christ who know who He is even in the midst of their pain. They are those who are certain of His identity even in the midst of their suffering.

This world will be changed by the manifest sons and daughters of God. It will not be changed by those who think, hope, aspire or wish—but those who *know* that Jesus is the Messiah, the Son of the living God. No matter what you are going through or how muddy your mess, I dare you to open your mouth and shout, "Jesus, I know who You are!"

You are my Savior.

You are my Deliverer.

You are my Healer.

You are my Rock.

You are my Redeemer.

You are my going in, and You are my going out.

You are my purpose.

You are my passion, and You are my promise.

Like Martha, you can worship in the midst of your wounding. She came to vent and ended up worshiping. She came to talk about her problem, but she ended up praising Him. It is easy to worship when all is well. It is easy to praise when everything is awesome.

Yet there exists a special remnant just like Martha who know that God is worthy of worship even when we are wounded, that God is worthy of praise even in our pain. Job, someone else renowned for seeking God in his suffering, said it this way: "I came naked from my mother's womb, and I will be naked when I leave. The LORD gave me what I had, and the LORD has taken it away. Praise the name of the LORD!" (Job 1:21 NLT).

No matter what or who you have lost, no matter how intense your pain, no matter how frustrated and frazzled you may be, you can still choose to worship and praise God. Habakkuk said,

> Even though the fig trees have no blossoms, and there are no grapes on the vines; even though the olive crop fails, and the fields lie empty and barren; even though the flocks die in the fields, and the cattle barns are empty, yet I will rejoice in the LORD! I will be joyful in the God of my salvation!
>
> Habakkuk 3:17–18 NLT

Are you willing to worship and give glory to God with tears rolling down your cheeks? Will you worship God in the valley and on the mountaintop? Can you praise Jesus in the desert and in the Promised Land? Could you rejoice in God's promises through the process and in the outcome?

Martha did not stay in the house. Martha did not stay in the atmosphere of mourning. She left her surroundings. There are people like Martha who go through brokenness but do not stay in brokenness. They go through hell, but hell does not go through them. People with Martha's faith declare, "My wounds will never stop my worship. My wounds are temporary, but my worship is permanent. My pain is for a season, but my praise is forever."

The tension lies in the divine dilemma of whether or not you will worship Him with your wounds and praise Him even in the midst of your pain. This miracle is not just about the resurrection of Lazarus. It is about wounded worshipers who refuse to let their pain kill their faith.

And this is what Jesus said about His worshipers: "God is spirit, and his worshipers must worship in the Spirit and in truth" (John 4:24).

When you worship in Spirit and in truth, you worship even when you are wounded.

When you worship in Spirit and in truth, you worship even when you are in pain.

When you worship in Spirit and in truth, you worship even when Jericho's walls stand in your way.

When you worship in Spirit and in truth, you worship even when you are surrounded by all the enemies of your purpose.

When you worship in Spirit and in truth, you worship in front of the giant that mocks you.

When you worship in Spirit and in truth, you worship in the midst of a fiery furnace.

When you worship in Spirit and in truth, you worship inside the jail house right after you have been beaten.

When you worship in Spirit and in truth, you worship after you have lost the person you love.

Because God is greater than anything you are going through. God is greater than your pain. God is greater than your worship.

Double Blind

I am convinced that God sometimes covers our eyes now in order for us to open them later for what is next. When Jesus healed the man blind from birth, He spit on the ground and made mud, which He then spread over the blind man's eyes (see John 9:6). In essence, Jesus blinded him to his own blindness. He placed the messy mask of the miraculous over this man's eyes in order to help him see the glory of God waiting for him ahead. In order to experience the tension of your holy mess, you must adjust your vision. Take your eyes off today's problems and open your eyes to tomorrow's promises.

IN ORDER TO EXPERIENCE THE TENSION OF YOUR HOLY MESS, YOU MUST ADJUST YOUR VISION.

This blind man engaged in a double-blind study and walked without hesitation with his mess ongoing. In a scientific double-blind study, neither participants nor researchers know which subjects are in the test groups and which are in the control groups. When you experience loss, injury, betrayal or disease, you feel powerless and uncertain of how to go forward. You wonder if God knows what He is doing; if He understands the depths of your pain. And if so, then why has He permitted this to happen? You feel as though you are caught in a double blind, unable to see your present and unable to see your future.

But sometimes you have to go *through* to get *to*.

Sometimes you have to walk with your mess to get to your miracle.

Sometimes you have to experience what feels like death before you rise again as Lazarus did, even though you will come out of your tomb and throw off your grave clothes.

It feels messy and awkward and uncomfortable when you are coming back to life walking in the mess to get to your miracle. But there is an expiration date on what you are going through. "For our present troubles are small and won't last very long. Yet they produce

for us a glory that vastly outweighs them and will last forever!"
(2 Corinthians 4:17 NLT).

When your praise speaks louder than your pain, nothing can
stop you.

When your integrity is more important than your influence,
nothing can stop you.

When you are driven by anointing rather than ambition, nothing can stop you.

When your hunger for righteousness is greater than your fear
of criticism, nothing can stop you.

When what is behind you is under the blood of Jesus, what is
in front of you cannot be stopped.

Sometimes it gets messy right before your miracle. When you
open your eyes, you may momentarily get mud in them. *So it is
time to wash them clean!*

——— OPEN YOUR EYES ———

As you have grown accustomed by now, use the questions below to help you process and apply the powerful principles in this chapter. Then spend some time opening your heart before God and choosing to praise Him in the midst of whatever pain you may be carrying. Do not hold back on what you are feeling even as you choose, as the blind man or Martha did, to worship in the midst of your wounding.

1. What are some of the false beliefs and inaccurate assumptions that cause you to struggle in blindness? How has God's truth illuminated the subjective bias of these false beliefs?

2. When have you experienced the miraculous power of God's Spirit only to encounter an even messier situation than before? How do you usually respond when life gets messier?

3. Will you dare to worship God even when you are wounded? Will you persist in praising Him even when your pain feels unbearable?

Dear God, my heart feels so heavy sometimes. I want to trust You and walk by faith, but then my emotions overwhelm me and cloud my vision. Open my eyes, Lord, so that I can see the holy mess of how You are working in my life. I know that I am a work in progress, and I praise You for loving me in the midst of my muddy messes. I am ready for You to wipe away the mud so that I can be cleansed and see with more clarity than ever before. Thank You for the way You redirect my gaze from the present problems to tomorrow's promises. In Jesus' name, Amen.

Wash Up

Open Your Eyes to Clean Obedience

God is looking for people who trust Him more than He is looking for those who understand Him.

Faith is trusting God enough to obey Him now and prepare for your next.

When it comes to cleanliness, water is essential. Water allows us to wash our bodies, which affords us a multitude of benefits. There is the hygienic and medical benefit of eliminating dirt, grime, germs and bacteria from our skin, hair and nails. Many people appreciate the effects that water, whether hot or cold, has on their circulation and overall health. Others like the way water can stimulate and awaken their senses, while others enjoy the way water can relax them.

There is also the social and relational benefit of looking and, perhaps more importantly, smelling clean and pleasant. Usually starting around puberty, most people learn that showering and bathing on a frequent basis makes them more appealing and socially acceptable to their peers. While other cultural factors influence one's bathing habits, the desire to fit in and be seen in a positive light contributes to our grooming and personal hygiene.

The psychological benefits of bathing are likely related to an awareness of both the health and social advantages. When camping or traveling in remote areas of the world, showering, let alone hot water, is often a luxury. After an intense workout or a day spent gardening, the feeling of water cascading over our body provides physical as well as emotional pleasure. Simply put, most people like feeling clean even if how or how often they achieve cleanliness varies.

I admit that I have never been much of a bath kind of guy. While I appreciate the conceptual idea of a nice large tub of hot sudsy water complete with candles burning and sandalwood soap scenting the air, I have never been patient enough to give myself to such an indulgent experience. Maybe it is my engineering mind, but showers seem much more efficient for the time invested. And after a long run, nothing beats a hot shower.

Cleaning our bodies is not the only benefit of bathing with water. According to the Bible, the cleansing power of water is also spiritual.

Learn to Discern

Throughout the pages of Scripture, water is used to wash, restore, hydrate, grow and transform. In the Old Testament we see Noah obey God and survive the Flood while Elijah endured a drought through God's provision. In the New Testament we find Jesus (and Peter, briefly) walking on water, as well as Paul being shipwrecked and washing up on the island of Malta.

We also find water used to wash away the miraculous mud from the eyes of the man blind since birth. After spitting on the ground, making mud and applying a mask of it over the man's eyes, Jesus told him to "wash in the Pool of Siloam" (John 9:7). John's account of this messy miracle also informs us that Siloam means *sent*, as in the water sent forth into this pool. But the pool's name is no coincidence because Jesus sent this man out to complete his miracle, and the man obeyed—and came home seeing. Instead of existing as if his life was washed up, this man washed up and saw the new life before him.

What is the difference between being washed up and washing up? *Obedience!*

Keep in mind that this man was not only blind but doubly so with mud covering his eyes. He could not see Jesus, but he could hear His voice. In that moment the blind man realized that who speaks into you is way more important than who speaks about you. Most likely, this man had been talked about since birth. People probably pitied him, bullied him, shunned him and ignored him.

WHAT IS THE DIFFERENCE BETWEEN BEING WASHED UP AND WASHING UP? OBEDIENCE!

And now this remarkable stranger had done the most peculiar thing. He spit to create mud and then placed it over his eyes. As if this behavior were not enough, the stranger then instructed him to go to the nearby Pool of Siloam, a local landmark familiar to him, and wash. Archaeological discoveries in recent decades indicate that the Pool of Siloam was likely fed by spring waters and used for ritual bathing.[1] So Jesus' instruction to go there and wash probably seemed logical to the blind man.

But even if Jesus' command surprised or confused the blind man, he did not question it. He obeyed. And he was healed.

Knowing the sound of our Shepherd's voice is vitally important if we want to experience the fulfillment of our messy miracles in life. Jesus said, "My sheep listen to my voice; I know them, and they follow me" (John 10:27). Our Lord reminded us that whoever has your ear will inevitably have your heart. When we are young and immature, we usually worry about who is talking about us. We care about what they think, what they say and how they are influencing others.

As we mature and grow wiser, however, we learn not to care about what others may say about us. We learn to care about whom we allow to speak into our lives. We learn to guard our hearts and minds in order to take our thoughts captive to Christ so that we may focus on matters of the Spirit. We realize that we cannot grant heart access to just anyone. We learn to discern.

Do not grant everyone access to your prayers. Do not grant everyone access to your dreams. Do not grant everyone access to your wounds. Access should be limited to people of integrity who can handle both the blessed and the broken you. Do not give everyone your ear.

Stop listening to unholy voices. Stop listening to toxic voices. Stop listening to gossiping voices. Stop listening to drama-filled voices. Stop listening to wounded voices. *Because wounded voices say broken things.*

FAITH IS TRUSTING GOD WHEN LIFE MAKES NO SENSE.

You do not need to understand God, and you do not need to make sense of God. You need to *trust* God. You need to *obey* God. God is looking for people who trust Him instead of those who understand Him. Faith is trusting God when life makes no sense. What you hear in the Spirit is more important than what you see in the flesh.

Jesus told the blind man, "Go wash yourself!" Again, we know Christ could have healed this man instantly, so why spit, make mud, cover his eyes and then tell him to go wash himself in the Pool of Sent? Because there are things you must do by yourself, for yourself. Yes, it is good if someone can help, but sometimes in life you have to learn to:

Pray for yourself.

Praise by yourself.

Lay hands on yourself.

Prophesy to yourself.

Rebuke yourself.

Celebrate yourself.

Anoint yourself.

You cannot ride others' coattails to praise the one healing you. You cannot jump on the bandwagon of someone else's breakthrough. There are decisions you cannot delegate. There are actions you cannot appropriate.

Go wash yourself. *Do your part to complete the miracle God is working in your life.*

Wash Your Sins Away

One of the ways we practice clean obedience is through baptism—using water to show others that we are born again in Christ through the power of the Holy Spirit. Once you have invited Jesus into your life and welcomed His Spirit into your heart, the next step of baptism demonstrates your commitment to God. The Bible tells us, "We know that we have come to know him if we keep his commands" (1 John 2:3). And Jesus instructed His followers to baptize new believers when He gave us the Great Commission: "Therefore go and make disciples of all nations, baptizing them in the name of the Father and of the Son and of the Holy Spirit" (Matthew 28:19).

Throughout the Bible, baptism is mentioned (27 times by my count) as a reflection of knowing God, and it occurs *after* you initiate your relationship by inviting Him into all areas of your life. "Those who accepted his message were baptized, and about three thousand were added to their number that day" (Acts 2:41).

Baptism as an act by itself does not secure your salvation—accepting God's free gift of grace through His Son, Jesus, secures your salvation and allows you to know God. The Bible tells us, however, to let others know about our relationship with Christ. Jesus said, "Whoever acknowledges me before others, I will also acknowledge before my Father in heaven. But whoever disowns me before others, I will disown before my Father in heaven" (Matthew 10:32–33).

Baptism shows everyone around you that you belong to God and that you are passionate about knowing Him, that you are following the example of Jesus and that you are being guided by the Holy Spirit.

> And this water symbolizes baptism that now saves you also—not the removal of dirt from the body but the pledge of a clear conscience toward God. It saves you by the resurrection of Jesus Christ, who has gone into heaven and is at God's right hand—with angels, authorities and powers in submission to him.
>
> 1 Peter 3:21–22

Jesus considered baptism important enough to ask His cousin John the Baptist to baptize Him in the Jordan River before starting His public ministry (see Matthew 3:13–15). His action resulted in an outpouring of the Spirit and affirmation from His Father: "As soon as Jesus was baptized, he went up out of the water. At that moment heaven was opened, and he saw the Spirit of God descending like a dove and alighting on him. And a voice from heaven said, 'This is my Son, whom I love; with him I am well pleased'" (verses 16–17).

When the apostle Paul shared his testimony with those in the early Church, he recalled the life-changing encounter he had with Christ when Paul was known as Saul, a relentless persecutor of Christians. Saul was struck blind and fasted for three days until God instructed a believer named Ananias to heal Saul and instruct him on next steps: "The God of our ancestors has chosen you. . . . You will be his witness to all people of what you have seen and heard. And now what are you waiting for? Get up, be baptized and wash your sins away, calling on his name'" (Acts 22:14–16).

Baptism by water remains a powerful demonstration of clean obedience.

Guess Who Came to Dinner

But baptism is not the only symbolic use for water. In two striking instances depicted in Scripture, we see how washing the feet of others with water demonstrates humility, service and compassion. The first example occurred when Jesus was having dinner at the home of a Pharisee. Apparently, word traveled fast because an unexpected visitor crashed the party.

> A woman in that town who lived a sinful life learned that Jesus was eating at the Pharisee's house, so she came there with an alabaster jar of perfume. As she stood behind him at his feet weeping, she began to wet his feet with her tears. Then she wiped them with her hair, kissed them and poured perfume on them.
>
> Luke 7:37–38

What a stunning display of humility, brokenness and gratitude. This woman, known by her sinful reputation, dared to show up uninvited at the home of a devout Jewish religious leader. Her belief that Jesus was indeed the Messiah compelled her to perform an intimate act of subservience usually delegated to household slaves. Instead of water from a basin, however, this woman used her own tears to wash the feet of Jesus. To complete her sacrificial gift, she dried the Master's feet with her hair before soothing and scenting them with wildly expensive perfume.

Her bold act of service was not appreciated by the host of the dinner party, however, who then denounced Jesus by association.

When the Pharisee who had invited him saw this, he said to himself, "If this man were a prophet, he would know who is touching him and what kind of woman she is—that she is a sinner." Jesus answered him, "Simon, I have something to tell you." "Tell me, teacher," he said. "Two people owed money to a certain moneylender. One owed him five hundred denarii, and the other fifty. Neither of them had the money to pay him back, so he forgave the debts of both. Now which of them will love him more?" Simon replied, "I suppose the one who had the bigger debt forgiven." "You have judged correctly," Jesus said. Then he turned toward the woman and said to Simon, "Do you see this woman? I came into your house. You did not give me any water for my feet, but she wet my feet with her tears and wiped them with her hair. You did not give me a kiss, but this woman, from the time I entered, has not stopped kissing my feet. You did not put oil on my head, but she has poured perfume on my feet. Therefore, I tell you, her many sins have been forgiven—as her great love has shown. But whoever has been forgiven little loves little." Then Jesus said to her, "Your sins are forgiven." The other guests began to say among themselves, "Who is this who even forgives sins?" Jesus said to the woman, "Your faith has saved you; go in peace."

Luke 7:39–50

The contrast between the woman of ill repute and the Pharisee, whom Jesus addresses as Simon, could not be sharper. She knows the weight of her sinfulness and thus feels immense gratitude to the One who can forgive her. Simon, who had invited Jesus to dinner but had failed to show true hospitality, becomes judgmental and self-righteous. The woman washing Jesus' feet with her tears shows us how to come clean in obedience—by praising and worshiping our God.

> **WHEN WE REALIZE THE DEBT OF GRATITUDE WE OWE TO CHRIST, WE HAVE NO CHOICE BUT TO WORSHIP.**

When we realize the debt of gratitude we owe to Christ, when we experience God's grace and forgiveness of our sins, when we recognize the power of the Holy Spirit in us—we have no choice but to worship.

Belief in the Blessing

Notice any similarities between this dinner-party scene and the one encountered by the blind man after Jesus healed him?

In both instances, the Pharisees and Jewish religious elite questioned and criticized those participating. They rebuked the newly sighted man when he called them out on their condemnation of Jesus as a sinner. And their opinion of this woman washing Jesus' feet seems to be just as low. In both cases, these religious leaders called Jesus a sinner for demonstrating His power as the Son of God—when, irony upon irony, He who is sinless forgave the sins of others.

And in both of these scenes, Jesus confirmed His identity to the participants while making the hypocrisy of the Pharisees crystal clear. You will recall that after the blind man was healed, the Jewish religious leaders interrogated that man twice and even called in his parents to testify. Then when the man confronted them, they insulted him and had him thrown out. But his story was not over—because that is when it came full circle:

> Jesus heard that they had thrown him out, and when he found him, he said, "Do you believe in the Son of Man?" "Who is he, sir?" the man asked. "Tell me so that I may believe in him." Jesus said, "You have now seen him; in fact, he is the one speaking with you." Then the man said, "Lord, I believe," and he worshiped him. Jesus said, "For judgment I have come into this world, so that the blind will see and those who see will become blind." Some Pharisees who were with him heard him say this and asked, "What? Are we blind too?" Jesus said, "If you were blind, you would not be guilty of sin; but now that you claim you can see, your guilt remains."
>
> John 9:35–41

Like the woman washing Jesus' feet, the newly sighted man chose to believe—and consequently, to worship. In his rebuttal to the Pharisees' interrogation, the man had already shown the only logical conclusion to draw about the One who healed him. Only through the power of God could anyone perform such a miracle.

Intellectual consent, however, is not the same as belief transformed into faith. Notice that when Jesus heard this man had been thrown out by the Pharisees, He went and found him. The man had demonstrated his obedience by washing and completing the miracle Jesus performed. The man had also revealed his loyalty and cognitive assessment of what happened to him when he testified before the Pharisees.

All that was left was to believe and to worship.

Belief in the Brokenness

For the man who was born blind, what a difference a day made—and what a roller-coaster ride of emotions he must have experienced. There he was, perhaps begging just outside the temple gates, like any other day in his world of darkness. Then suddenly a stranger stopped to make a mud pie and infuse it with divine power to heal. Obeying the instruction to go wash in the Pool of Siloam, he splashed his eyes over and over in the cool, clear water. When he wiped them dry, he could do something he had never done before in his life—he could see!

Keep in mind how bizarre this entire experience must have been. He had no logical, human-based reason to do what this man told him to do. After growing up and becoming an adult without his sight, why in the world would he dare to believe that anything—or anyone—could change his plight?

I cannot help but wonder if this man sowed the seeds of his belief by choosing to obey. He was willing to receive the miracle in the mud literally spread before his eyes. Later, after going through the metaphorical mud, or what we might call something more impolite, this man voiced his faith when Jesus revealed Himself in front of the man's now-functioning eyes. His belief was planted in the mud, but it blossomed in the miracle.

HIS BELIEF WAS PLANTED IN THE MUD, BUT IT BLOSSOMED IN THE MIRACLE.

Belief in the dark and broken places of our lives seems to invite God's miraculous power. Once again, the healing of Lazarus' cold and lifeless body in the tomb comes to my mind. Returning to that emotionally charged scene between Jesus, who had allowed His beloved friend to die, and Martha, the loving sister of the deceased, we see that belief highlights the beauty of resurrection power in action:

Jesus told her, "I am the resurrection and the life. Anyone who believes in me will live, even after dying. Everyone who lives in me and believes in me will never ever die. Do you believe this, Martha?" "Yes, Lord," she told him. "I have always believed you are the Messiah, the Son of God, the one who has come into the world from God."

John 11:25–27 NLT

Martha was broken but she still believed. Jesus emphasized the power of faith, of believing in what appeared to be impossible, time and time again. The message emerged on multiple occasions: If you believe, you are healed. If you believe, you are forgiven. If you believe, you are blessed. The message resounds for you today: *You are what you believe!*

If you want to live out your God-ordained purpose,
    if you want to fulfill your assignment on this planet,
    if you want to live in abundant life,
    then you must believe.
It is not about what you feel; it is about what you believe.
It is not about what you hope; it is about what you believe.
It is not about theory; it is about belief.
It is not a hypothesis; it is about belief.
It is not a supposition; it is about belief.
It is not theoretical; it is about belief.

We must believe even in the midst of brokenness. We must believe even in the face of a broken world. Bombs descend upon children, but we still believe. Discord and strife flourish in America, but we still believe. Inflation rates are climbing while finances are dwindling, but we still believe. More than ever, we must believe. What do we believe?

> We believe in God, the Father Almighty, Creator of heaven and earth.
> We believe in Jesus Christ, His only Son, our Lord.
> We believe Jesus is the only Way, the Truth and the Life.
> He was conceived by the power of the Holy Spirit
> and born of the Virgin Mary.
> He suffered under Pontius Pilate,
> was crucified, died and was buried.
> He descended to the dead.
> On the third day, He rose again.
> He ascended into heaven
> and is seated at the right hand of the Father.
> He will come again to judge the living and the dead.
> We believe in the Holy Spirit,
> the holy Church,
> the communion of saints,
> the forgiveness of sins,
> the resurrection of the body,
> and the life everlasting. Amen.

This is the divine bill of rights for every believer. But through the power of the Holy Spirit in our lives, there is also an amendment to what we believe. Through the promises of God's Word and the power of His Spirit, we believe a derivative, tangential and itemized list that cannot and will not be denied.

> We believe that through the Lord Jesus Christ, our homes will
> be saved.
> We believe that our children and our children's children will
> walk upon the ruins of what we bring down in this generation.

We believe that all of God's promises are yes and amen.

We believe that the latter glory will be greater than the former glory.

We believe that Jesus still saves.

We believe that Jesus still delivers.

We believe that Jesus is still healing.

And we believe that Jesus is coming back again.

Blessed to Be a Blessing

When you believe, your obedience follows without question. When you receive God's blessings, when you experience a messy miracle through the power of His Spirit, when you open your eyes and see His goodness, obedience is simple. You know He loves you and that the plans He has for you are good and filled with hope. You know He died on the cross for you so that you might be forgiven and enjoy eternal life with Him in heaven. When you wash away the mud from your miracle, you want others to see Him, too.

When you obey God by giving Him your praise and worship, you want to serve Him by showing others who He is and how much He loves them, too. You want to fulfill your God-given purpose and lead by example even as you serve in humility. And that is exactly what we see in the other example of water that was used to wash someone's feet. Only in this instance, the roles were reversed because Jesus was the One doing the washing.

After having spent three years together doing public ministry, teaching, healing and traveling together, Jesus and His disciples had precious little time left to spend together prior to His death. Even though He knew He would see them after His resurrection, Christ wanted to make their final meal together more than memorable. He wanted to demonstrate the extent of His humility in serving them. He wanted to set an example for them (and us).

It was just before the Passover Festival. Jesus knew that the hour had come for Him to leave this world and go to the Father. Having loved His own who were in the world, He loved them to the end.

The evening meal was in progress, and the devil had already prompted Judas, the son of Simon Iscariot, to betray Jesus. Jesus knew that the Father had put all things under his power, and that he had come from God and was returning to God; so he got up from the meal, took off his outer clothing, and wrapped a towel around his waist. After that, he poured water into a basin and began to wash his disciples' feet, drying them with the towel that was wrapped around him. He came to Simon Peter, who said to him, "Lord, are you going to wash my feet?" Jesus replied, "You do not realize now what I am doing, but later you will understand." "No," said Peter, "you shall never wash my feet." Jesus answered, "Unless I wash you, you have no part with me." "Then, Lord," Simon Peter replied, "not just my feet but my hands and my head as well!" Jesus answered, "Those who have had a bath need only to wash their feet; their whole body is clean. And you are clean, though not every one of you." For he knew who was going to betray him, and that was why he said not every one was clean. When he had finished washing their feet, he put on his clothes and returned to his place. "Do you understand what I have done for you?" he asked them. "You call me 'Teacher' and 'Lord,' and rightly so, for that is what I am. Now that I, your Lord and Teacher, have washed your feet, you also should wash one another's feet. I have set you an example that you should do as I have done for you. Very truly I tell you, no servant is greater than his master, nor is a messenger greater than the one who sent him. Now that you know these things, you will be blessed if you do them."

John 13:2–17

I suspect that I do not have to describe for you how nasty twelve pairs of adult male feet can be. And these were feet most likely caked with mud, dirt, sand and dust, not to mention sweat and who-knows-what from the walkways of Jerusalem. But that is the point Jesus wanted to make to His followers, then and now: if we follow His example, then we must be willing to do what needs doing. He told them that no servant is greater than his master, no messenger greater than the originator of the message.

As you experience the power of God's Spirit transforming your mess into His miracle, you have even more to share with those around you. You are blessed to be a blessing. When you wash away the muddy residue of your past, you open your eyes to your new future. You open your eyes with the ability to lead others to the Source of your healing.

Get Ready to See

When you are washed clean in the blood of the Lamb, your eyes are opened to what is next. Washing restores your vision for the future God has for you. Remaining clean and obedient now prepares you for your miracle during your mess. Job, another believer in the midst of his brokenness and his blessing, declared, "My ears had heard of you but now my eyes have seen you" (Job 42:5).

You have heard the truth of the Gospel, my friend. Now get ready to see the power of the Spirit transform your life.

Get ready to see God detox your relationships, sanitize your surroundings and vaccinate your future.

Get ready to see your nation embraced by the Father, redeemed by the Son and filled with the Holy Spirit.

Get ready to see a people on the brink of revival.

Get ready to see a community ripe for signs, wonders, healings and miracles.

Get ready to see young men and women leading an awakening where righteousness and justice inundate every sphere of society.

Get ready to see God's children getting ready for the coming of the Lord.

You do not see failure—you see victory.

You do not see victims—you see conquerors.

You do not see Pharaohs, Goliaths, Jezebels and Herods—you see Elijahs and Elishas, Ruths and Deborahs, Joshuas and Peters and Pauls.

You see prophets, evangelists, pastors, teachers, exhorters and miracle workers.

You see doctors, lawyers, teachers, politicians, businesspeople, artists, creators, innovators, entrepreneurs, actors and entertainers, singers and dancers committed to Christ and filled with the Holy Spirit.

You see children casting out devils.

You see young men and women prophesying and healing.

You see the emerging generation having visions.

You see the older generation having dreams.

You see the name of Jesus lifted high.

So open your eyes and look all around you.

Get ready to see the love of God, the truth of God, the grace of God, the power of God and the glory of God as you have never seen before. Get ready to see the favor, the overflow and the abundance of God as you have never seen before.

When Jesus is your Lord,

when you are full of His Holy Spirit,
when you walk in His promises,
when you adhere to His Word,
you begin to prepare now for your next.
Your next is about revelation.
Your now is about sowing.
Your next is about reaping.
Your now is your test.
Your next is your testimony.
Your now is the battle.
Your next is the breakthrough.
Your now is about faith.
Your next is about favor.
Your now is about order.
Your next is about overflow.

Your now is not your next, but what you do now will determine what you see next!

What you say now,
what you pray now,
what you praise now,
what you love now,
what you forgive now,
what you bind now,
what you release now,
what you confess now,
what you hold on to now,
what you surrender now,
what you declare now,
what you read now,
what you focus on now will determine what you see next.
Wash your eyes and open them to see God's power in action!

───── OPEN YOUR EYES ─────

Even when you love the Lord passionately and faithfully, obedience can still feel challenging at times. While the choice to obey is often simple, living out obedience can be difficult. But those moments are opportunities to strengthen your faith and experience more of God's power in your life. When you feel weak, the power of the Holy Spirit sustains you and empowers you to do what you could not do alone. No matter what you may be going through, you must believe that God is at work producing your miracle in the midst of what appears to be a muddy mess.

Wipe away the mud and drench yourself in the power of the Spirit. As you do, the questions below can help you reorient your vision. After quieting your heart before the Lord, spend a few minutes in prayer asking Him to meet you right where you are. Just as Jesus sought out the just-healed man who had been blind from birth, He is revealing Himself before you. Whether you are feeling broken or blessed, or likely a blend of both, just believe and worship.

1. When have you struggled with being obedient to God's Word and the leading of His Spirit most recently? How did you handle your hesitation?
2. What miracles have you experienced in your life that help sustain your faith and strengthen your

trust in God? How has the Lord opened your eyes to His power through these experiences?

3. What gives you strength to persevere and live by faith when your circumstances appear to close in on you? What is God speaking into your life right now?

Dear Lord, I give You all praise, honor and glory for the miracles You are performing right now in the midst of my messes. Thank You for pursuing me when I feel uncertain and outcast from those who refuse to see Your hand at work in my life. I believe You are the Way, the Truth and the Life, and I see Your power at work more clearly than ever before. Continue to strengthen my faith when obstacles loom and miracles seem impossible to imagine. Shine through me, God, so that others can see Your love for them and Your power to change lives. In Jesus' name, Amen.

Look Again

Open Your Eyes and Worship Jesus

When you experience God's miracle in your mess, look again at what you see.

Unconditional worship is the only appropriate response when you open the eyes of your heart.

M any people believe they can immediately spot counterfeit merchandise.

I used to be one of them. After all, I have walked down Canal Street in New York before and seen the dozens of street vendors with their knock-off luxury items spread on blankets and card tables. I have traveled overseas and have walked by open-air market stalls and small shops advertising name-brand luxury items at deep-discount prices.

At first glance, you see all kinds of designer purses, sunglasses, caps, jewelry and watches for a fraction of their usual retail price. Upon closer inspection, though, many of the logos and labels seem a little off. The colors are close but not exact, and the craftsmanship of the originals is clearly lacking. Anyone who knows what the real items look like would not be fooled for long.

But then I was in a meeting one afternoon and noticed the new watch my friend was wearing. My first thought was that he must be wealthier than I had realized, that he had just won the lottery or that he had received some other windfall. I am not a big watch guy, especially now that our phones can inform us of the time so alarmingly well, but the sleek chronometer on my friend's wrist made me reconsider. The gleaming stainless-steel bracelet and black dial easily identified the Swiss maker of his major bling.

After the meeting, we had coffee together and discussed the presentation we had just witnessed. As we finished our beverages, I complimented him on his watch and gently teased him about its exorbitant value.

"Thanks, Sam," he said. "Here, take a look if you'd like." And before I could decline, he took the watch off and handed it to me. Once again, I had to admire the mechanical artistry of the timepiece. The symmetry of the numerals, the discreet date window, the iconic shape of the hands—the details screamed well-made and expensive.

"Why don't you try it on?" he urged, seeing my admiration. I smiled and shook my head.

"Get thee behind me," I joked and handed it back. "I'm afraid I'd drop it or accidentally scratch the crystal." My friend held the watch and then tapped it—facedown—on the tabletop.

"Nah, can't hurt this baby. It's indestructible. Plus, it's not that expensive and can easily be replaced."

My eyes widened. "Perhaps for your income bracket, my friend."

He smiled knowingly, then began laughing. "Sam, it's not real. It's just a really good knockoff. Bought it from a guy I know in Singapore."

"No way!" I said as I picked up the watch again. "I don't know much about watches, but I can spot quality. And I would never guess this isn't the real deal."

"The real deal is crazy-expensive—way more than I feel comfortable spending on something like this for myself. But when my friend offered it to me for the price of a Timex, I couldn't resist."

"Well, you definitely fooled me."

My friend shrugged. "It uses a lot of the same materials as the original, but if you opened up the case and compared the mechanism, that's where you couldn't miss the difference. Sometimes a counterfeit looks just like the original it's imitating. But it's never the same inside."

Counterfeit Faith

The word *counterfeit* came into the English language in the thirteenth century from both French and Anglo usage to describe items—often works of art or expensive household items—created specifically to imitate or at least resemble items already available. The two parts of the word have Latinate roots, with *counter* meaning "against" and *feit* meaning "something made or created."[1] Literally, a counterfeit goes against an original creation, making it synonymous with the word *imitation*.

In most cases, however, this kind of imitation is not the sincerest form of flattery. And counterfeiting is not limited to monetary currency and luxury items. According to *Fast Company*, recent studies estimate that almost *one trillion* dollars' worth of counterfeit merchandise changes hands each year in the global economy.[2]

And with the advent of online shopping, heralded by Amazon, for virtually all personal and household products, fake products have infiltrated almost all consumer goods, not just luxury items. From laundry detergent to baby formula, products are sold by counterfeiters who sell their wares using well-known brands and labels but with cheaper, inferior ingredients. To combat these practices and protect its customers, Amazon formed a Counterfeit Crimes Unit in 2020 that has blocked more than ten billion fraudulent listings and destroyed two million counterfeit products.[3] Counterfeiting is obviously a major criminal and economic problem that touches millions of lives. Many consumers have no clue they are purchasing fake products.

But I suspect spiritual counterfeiting is also a major issue in our world today. In fact, based on what we see in the Bible, there is nothing new about people faking their faith. Self-righteousness, legalism and hypocrisy have been around for thousands of years.

Returning to the miraculously messy encounter Jesus had with the man who had been born blind, we find the Jewish religious leaders trying to discredit the recipient of this divine miracle. They were also trying to paint Christ as a sinner who was committing heresy. The religious leaders wanted to be seen as pious, devout followers of God but failed to recognize the Son of God in their midst. Greater still, they seemed frightened by the possibility that Jesus really could be the Messiah who had been promised by the prophets of old. Why? Because Jesus did not look or act like what they expected.

The Pharisees and Jewish religious leaders inherently expected a Messiah who recognized their earthly status and showed them the respect and admiration they thought they deserved. They followed all the Laws of Moses to the letter, prayed eloquently in public and openly judged and denounced sinners they encountered. These temple elitists justified their sinful actions by pointing out the actions of others, including dragging a woman who was caught amid an adulterous liaison before Jesus and bribing Judas to betray his Master.

And their motive was often to protect the veneer of their own counterfeit faith. They were not focused on pleasing God, obeying the essence of the law or using their power to serve others responsibly and charitably; instead, these phonies persecuted Jesus—and by association, those who believed in Him. People who were willing to place their trust in the power of God. People who were willing to set aside their expectations and take a second look. People who were willing to receive the miracle for them in the midst of their mess.

You Are Looking at Him

Even after the blind man had been healed and had testified twice before them, even after they dismissed him for daring to question their authority, the Jewish religious leaders seemingly refused to give up. Based on the end of this event that was recounted in the gospel of John, they appear to have followed him, or Jesus, or both. Like private eyes on a stakeout, they must have been eavesdropping on the post-miracle conversation Jesus had with the man He had healed earlier that day. Because based on their interruption, they clearly hoped to have the last word.

> Jesus heard that they had thrown him out, and went and found him. He asked him, "Do you believe in the Son of Man?" The man said, "Point him out to me, sir, so that I can believe in him." Jesus said, "You're looking right at him. Don't you recognize my voice?" "Master, I believe," the man said, and worshiped him. Jesus then said, "I came into the world to bring everything into the clear light of day, making all the distinctions clear, so that those who have never seen will see, and those who have made a great pretense of seeing will be exposed as blind." Some Pharisees overheard him and said, "Does that mean you're calling us blind?" Jesus said,

"If you were really blind, you would be blameless, but since you claim to see everything so well, you're accountable for every fault and failure."

John 9:35–41 MSG

When Jesus healed this man of his congenital blindness, the Lord demonstrated His ability to infuse His divine DNA into the dirt at His feet in order to create a mud-mask miracle. By choosing to perform the miracle in this fashion, Christ demonstrated the essence of His identity as both God and man, the bridge between heaven and earth, the divine incarnation of God in human form. But when the man He healed had been thrown out by the religious elite, Jesus went to find him.

Jesus did not have to go after this man any more than He needed to heal him in the first place. Aware of how this new recipient of miraculous sight had stood up to the Pharisees, Christ chose to reveal Himself to him in a direct, undeniable and unmistakable fashion. He asked the man point-blank, "Do you believe in the Son of Man?"

Rather than ask the man, "Do you believe in Me?" or "Do you believe in the Son of God?" Jesus referred to Himself as the Son of Man. This was a way of referring to Himself that He frequently used. By my count, we find "Son of Man" about eighty times in the New Testament, with thirty of those being in the gospel of Matthew. In addition to emphasizing the divinity of God in human form, "Son of Man" holds historical and scriptural significance.

Most Jewish listeners hearing these references would know that "Son of Man" appears a dozen times in the Old Testament, in both Ezekiel (see 2:1–10) and Daniel (see 7:13–14). These references call to mind the human suffering Jesus endured on our behalf. While fully God, He was also fully human and experienced all that we experience as human beings, yet without sinning (see Hebrews 4:15; 2 Corinthians 5:21). This duality of being God and man ultimately points to Jesus' purpose in coming to earth in human form: "For the Son of Man came to seek and to save the lost" (Luke 19:10).

The miracle man responded to Jesus' question in a very telling way. "Point him out to me, sir, so that I can believe in him." This man has been using his vision for less than 24 hours, and yet he still wanted Jesus to point out—literally, most likely—the Son of Man. Basically, he seems to be saying, "I want to believe. Just show me."

Jesus said, "You're looking right at Him. Don't you recognize My voice?" Notice the inference here. After relying his entire life on his sense of hearing, the man blind from birth had surely developed an acute ear for identifying people by their voices. So, in one sense, Jesus asked this based on recognizing His new follower's heightened auditory cognition.

But perhaps more significantly, Jesus also alluded to the logical conclusion this newly sighted man had presented to the religious leaders interrogating him. "Ever since the world began, no one has been able to open the eyes of someone born blind. If this man were not from God, he couldn't have done it" (John 9:32–33 NLT). So, by asking, "Don't you recognize My voice?" Jesus was also helping this man accept what he clearly already knew.

Miracles in Our Midst

Sometimes I suspect Jesus asks us the same question that He asked this once-blind man: "I am right in front of you. Don't you know My voice when you hear it?" Because when we follow our Good Shepherd, when we have the Holy Spirit living in us, we learn the sound of our Savior's voice as confidently as the miracle recipient heard it that day. Consider another occasion when Jesus stated, "My sheep listen to my voice; I know them, and they follow me. I give them eternal life, and they shall never perish; no one will snatch them out of my hand" (John 10:27–28).

When we are listening to and following the Spirit's voice, we learn to see Jesus all around us—in the stunning beauty of Creation, in the lives of other people and in the miracles in our midst. When we follow our Master's voice, we may need to take a second or a third look, but we cannot miss His presence right in front of us. As our spiritual eyes grow accustomed to looking through a divine lens and seeing God's eternal perspective, we realize there is so much more going on than meets our mortal eyes.

Because God is always at work in our lives, whether we see it—or see it the way we expect to see it—or not. Paul wrote to the early believers at Ephesus, "I pray that the eyes of your heart may be enlightened in order that you may know the hope to which he has called you, the riches of his glorious inheritance in his holy people, and his incomparably great power for us who believe" (Ephesians 1:18–19).

God's Word makes the contrast even sharper between what we see with our eyes and what we see with the eyes of our heart. "As we look not to the things that are seen but to the things that are unseen. For the things that are seen are transient, but the things that are unseen are eternal" (2 Corinthians 4:18 ESV). We learn to open our eyes and see beyond what our human eyes register as we mature in our faith. "For we walk by faith, not by sight" (2 Corinthians 5:7 ESV).

Even when we have been walking by faith and growing in the Lord, we can still take our eyes off Jesus and become overwhelmed by what we see. We are stepping out in faith and drawing closer to God than ever before despite the storms raging around us—when suddenly we stumble and lose our footing. Instead of walking on water, we are suddenly faltering in fear.

Just ask Peter.

Against the Wind

Of all Jesus' disciples in the New Testament, none intrigues me more than Simon Peter. A fisherman by trade, Peter displays both the conflicting emotions and the passionate faith that most followers of Jesus experience in their relationship with Him. After having drawn a blade to defend Jesus when the Roman soldiers came to arrest Him in the Garden of Gethsemane, Peter proceeded to deny even knowing Christ—not once but three times—only hours later. Perhaps the reason Peter intrigues me so much, though, emerges from his impaired vision.

I say this because of two different situations in which Peter shifted perspective and lost sight of the spiritual as he focused on the temporal. One may seem more obvious than the other. Peter and the disciples were boating one night when a storm came up. After teaching and feeding the five thousand–plus in attendance, Jesus sent His disciples ahead to the other side of the Sea of Galilee. He needed to spend some time in prayer alone (see Matthew 14). When Jesus finally tried to join them, Peter struggled with what he saw.

> Shortly before dawn Jesus went out to them, walking on the lake. When the disciples saw him walking on the lake, they were terrified. "It's a ghost," they said, and cried out in fear. But Jesus immediately said to them: "Take courage! It is I. Don't be afraid." "Lord, if it's you," Peter replied, "tell me to come to you on the water." "Come," he said. Then Peter got down out of the boat, walked on the water and came toward Jesus. But when he saw the wind, he was afraid and, beginning to sink, cried out, "Lord, save me!" Immediately

Jesus reached out his hand and caught him. "You of little faith," he said, "why did you doubt?" And when they climbed into the boat, the wind died down. Then those who were in the boat worshiped him, saying, "Truly you are the Son of God."

Matthew 14:25–33

The disciples thought they were seeing a ghost and reacted perhaps as any of us might respond. Remember that they were on a boat in the predawn moments of a dark, windy morning. Jesus told them not to be afraid because it was not a ghost they saw—"It is I." He assumed understandably that they would recognize His voice even if they could not see Him clearly. It is likely the same assumption Christ made when He asked the former blind man, "Don't you recognize My voice?"

We do not know if Peter and the others could not hear their Master clearly, but we do know that Peter still was not entirely convinced. He came up with an impromptu test that only Jesus could fulfill: "Lord, if it's You, tell me to come to You on the water." I find it striking that Peter did not ask for Jesus to prove Himself by illuminating His face, stopping the wind or hopping in their boat with them. Peter wanted Jesus to empower him to do what the Lord Himself was doing—walking on water.

Jesus commanded Peter to come out of the boat toward Him, and so Peter did just that. We are not told how many steps he took or how far he made it, but it did not take long for Peter to lose sight of his Master and to lose the supernatural power sustaining his footsteps on the waves. Why did Peter falter like this? We are told that "when he saw the wind, he was afraid and, beginning to sink, cried out" (Matthew 14:30).

Peter's experience here remains incredibly relatable for us today. When we are feeling uncertain, anxious and afraid, we ask God to give us a sign, to empower us to do something impossible. Then, when the Lord gives us His power, we step out of our boats and begin walking on water. Before long, though, just as Peter did, we see the wind. And what I love about this is that the wind really is not something we can see.

Just think about it. We see the wind move trees or blow across water or swirl dust in the air, but we cannot see the currents themselves. When we put ourselves in Peter's sandals, however, we know we do not have to see the wind to be afraid of how it feels all around us. When we choose to be a wind watcher, we allow ourselves to be overwhelmed by what our senses tell us. This is a natural human reaction to most adverse circumstances—but we still have a choice, just as Peter did. We can give in and live according to what our senses tell us, or we can continue walking by faith even when life gets harder.

> **WHEN WE CHOOSE TO BE A WIND WATCHER, WE ALLOW OURSELVES TO BE OVERWHELMED BY WHAT OUR SENSES TELL US.**

Sometimes we need to look again rather than look away.

Impaired Vision

The other time when Peter's impaired vision caused problems emerges not on a windy lake but in a conversation with Jesus. Here is the context: Early in Jesus' public ministry, He used divine discernment in revealing His identity as the Son of Man, similar to what we find with the blind man He healed. On one occasion, though, as Christ shared the implications of being God's Son, Peter struggled to grasp his Master's meaning:

> Jesus and his disciples left Galilee and went up to the villages near Caesarea Philippi. As they were walking along, he asked them,

"Who do people say I am?" "Well," they replied, "some say John the Baptist, some say Elijah, and others say you are one of the other prophets." Then he asked them, "But who do you say I am?" Peter replied, "You are the Messiah."

Mark 8:27–29 NLT

We are not told why Jesus asked His disciples who people said He was, but it is reasonable to assume He was aware that He was already attracting attention and inspiring rumors. Or perhaps Jesus simply wanted to make the contrast clear between rumors of His identity and the reality of His deity. Because when the disciples mentioned John the Baptist, Elijah or one of the prophets, Jesus then asked a much more personal and pertinent question: "But who do you say I am?"

Notice that Peter gave what seems to be the obvious answer: "You are the Messiah." But then their conversation took a surprising turn as Christ described what lay ahead for Him as the Messiah:

Then Jesus began to tell them that the Son of Man must suffer many terrible things and be rejected by the elders, the leading priests, and the teachers of religious law. He would be killed, but three days later he would rise from the dead. As he talked about this openly with his disciples, Peter took him aside and began to reprimand him for saying such things. Jesus turned around and looked at his disciples, then reprimanded Peter. "Get away from me, Satan!" he said. "*You are seeing things merely from a human point of view, not from God's.*" Then, calling the crowd to join his disciples, he said, "If any of you wants to be my follower, you must give up your own way, take up your cross, and follow me. If you try to hang on to your life, you will lose it. But if you give up your life for my sake and for the sake of the Good News, you will save it."

Mark 8:31–35 NLT, emphasis added

You cannot miss Peter's audacity here in reprimanding Jesus. Evidently, Peter's expectations regarding who Jesus was did not include suffering, rejection and crucifixion. From Peter's limited, human viewpoint, the Son of God would never have to endure such pain, injustice and abandonment from the people He came to save. Why? Because God is all-powerful and could easily destroy anyone who was attempting to harm Him during His time on earth.

Jesus then famously rebuked Peter about as harshly as possible: "Get away from me, Satan!" It was not that Peter was suddenly possessed by the devil—at least, I do not believe that is the case. But by reprimanding Jesus for foretelling what He had to face as the Son of Man, Peter reminded Jesus that His willingness to endure such abuse, such trauma, even death was, in fact, a choice. I believe this is the humanity of Jesus telling Peter not to tempt Him. By rebuking Peter in this manner, it is as if Christ was saying, "Don't remind Me that I could choose not to do My Father's will. I'm on a mission here and My mission cannot fail."

Peter failed to grasp Jesus' ability to foreknow the future into which He was to walk and, perhaps more importantly, its necessity for Jesus to pay for the sins of the world. As this passionate disciple experienced the power of Christ's Spirit in him, however, Peter became a champion of the Gospel message and was foundational to the early Church. He learned to grow by no longer seeing only through his eyes but through the eyes of his heart.

Unconditional Worship

This process of developing spiritual vision also happened for the blind man Jesus healed. Once Jesus revealed Himself as the Son of Man, how did the man respond? "'Master, I believe,' the man said, and worshiped him" (John 9:38 MSG). It is the same response the wind-tossed disciples had when they realized that it was really Jesus in their midst. They worshiped Him and declared, "Truly you are the Son of God" (Matthew 14:33).

Unconditional worship is the only appropriate response when you see Jesus!

Instead of worshiping Christ, however, the Pharisees heard the exchange between Jesus and the miracle man and asked, "Does that mean you're calling us blind?" (John 9:40 MSG). You can almost hear the contempt and indignation in their voices. But the truth of the One answering their question was not what they wanted to hear. "If you were really blind, you would be blameless, but since you claim to see everything so well, you're accountable for every fault and failure" (John 9:41 MSG).

UNCONDITIONAL WORSHIP IS THE ONLY APPROPRIATE RESPONSE WHEN YOU SEE JESUS!

Notice their fault lies in their claiming "to see everything so well," making them accountable for the "fault and failure" of their self-righteousness and hypocrisy. Instead of seeing Jesus for who He is, the Son of God, these unrepentant religious leaders saw only what they wanted to see—someone they feared and hated who was a threat to their power. They refused to look again and open their eyes. They remained blind while the man who had been born blind was granted double vision. He received the gift of healthy eyes and the gift of faith in the Giver of that gift.

I can only imagine that this man worshiped Jesus with love, praise and gratitude that would put many a church service to shame. This man knew when to stand up—before the Pharisees—and when to bow down—before Christ the Lord. This man learned to open his eyes and see, and who he saw resulted in worship. I daresay he did not care what the Pharisees thought of him or what they might do to him. All he cared about was worshiping Jesus.

When you experience the power, peace and joy in your messy miracle, you open your eyes and worship. You worship in the midst of your wounds, you rejoice in the midst of your ruckus and you praise through your problems. You sing in the desert because you know you will dance in the Promised Land. With the psalmist you proclaim, "Come, let us bow down in worship, let us kneel before the LORD our Maker" (Psalm 95:6).

When you bow before God, you can stand before man.

When you kneel with conviction, you can stand up to conquer.

When you begin the day on your knees, you will finish the day on your feet.

When you open your eyes to worship, God will reveal His presence anew.

God will bless you in the presence of those who broke you.

God will fill you in the presence of those who forsook you.

God will use you in the presence of those who refused you.

God will lift you up in the presence of those who brought you down.

God will promote you in the presence of those who persecuted you.

God will crown you in the presence of those who canceled you.

God will shine on you in the presence of those who shunned you.

The Bible assures us that faith comes from hearing the Word of God (see Romans 10:17). Now is not the time to listen to the Pharisees who doubt the power of Jesus even when they are confronted with the walking miracle you demonstrate in their midst. Now is not the time to listen to gossips and gabbers who speculate about who Jesus is when you already know He is the Son of God, the Prince of Peace, Emmanuel, the Messiah, your Lord and Savior. Now is not the time to look at the wind or listen to the voice of fear in your mind.

To whom have you been listening? Are there some voices you need to mute?

I will never forget being in Washington, DC, in 2017 on the day of the new president's inauguration. I was about to go up and speak before more than a billion people on television, social media and live streaming when—I kid you not—I received a new message on Facebook from some stranger warning me that she had a prophetic word that something terrible was about to happen. While I wanted to give her the benefit of the doubt, and while I hoped her motives were well-intended, what I knew was that God had performed nothing short of a miracle for me to be where I was that day, speaking and praying for our commander in chief before a global gathering.

So you know what I did? I blocked her! Her voice was unknown, so I had to listen to the voice I knew—the voice of my Shepherd. The voice of God's Spirit within me. The voice that the man who had been blind since birth recognized as his Healer and his Master. The voice that Peter heard say, "Come."

I knew then what I still know, and I want to make sure you know: "'No weapon formed against you shall prosper, and every tongue *which* rises against you in judgment you shall condemn. This *is* the heritage of the servants of the LORD, and their righteousness *is* from Me,' says the LORD" (Isaiah 54:17 NKJV).

No weapon formed against you will prosper.
No weapon formed against your family will prosper.

No weapon formed against your children will prosper.

No weapon formed against your faith will prosper.

No weapon formed against your future will prosper.

No weapon formed against your health will prosper.

No weapon formed against your generation will prosper.

No weapon formed against your worship will prosper.

My friend, do not open your eyes to prove your haters wrong. Do not open your eyes to prove your family wrong. Do not open your eyes to prove anything.

Your worship is more powerful than your wounding. Your testimony is more powerful than your trauma. Your praise is more powerful than your pain.

What Jesus did for you is greater than what hell did to you. What Jesus did for you is greater than what life did to you. What Jesus did for you is greater than what you did to yourself.

Refuse to settle for a counterfeit faith. Refuse to see with only your eyes. Refuse to second-guess the Maker of your miracles.

Open your eyes and worship the living God. Open your eyes and worship in the Spirit of Truth. *Open your eyes and worship the Lord Jesus Christ.*

——— OPEN YOUR EYES ———

Once more, use these questions and the prayer starter below as an opportunity to see Jesus more clearly, to hear the voice of His Spirit and to step out in faith. Eliminate as many distractions and interruptions as possible. Silence your phone, shut your laptop, close your screen and give God your full and undivided attention for the next few minutes. Your goal is simply to bask in the presence of your Father and to marvel at the miracles He is making from the messy mud in your life. In other words, open your eyes and worship.

1. Looking back over times when God has miraculously provided, healed and delivered you, what do you notice now that you could not see then?
2. When have you chosen to worship Jesus even during a painful situation or a traumatic event? How did you experience His presence even through your suffering?
3. What do you see when you look at your life through the eyes of your heart? What changes do you know God wants you to make in order to draw closer to Him?

Dear Lord, never allow me to take Your many gifts, blessings, signs, wonders and miracles for granted. Thank You for all the spiritual riches You pour into my life. I give You my praise and worship today and all the days of my life. May my life be a testimony of Your triumph over trials as I persevere through the power of Your Spirit and walk in faithful obedience. Open the eyes of my heart, God, so that I may see everything and everyone the way You see them. Help me to look beyond the tangible and temporal in order to focus on the invisible and eternal. In Jesus' name, Amen.

No-Secret Identity

Open Your Eyes to Who You Are in Christ

You are no longer who you once were.

In Jesus, through Jesus, with Jesus, because of Jesus, the new you is alive and well!

My boyhood heroes did not have secret identities—they had *reputations*.

Growing up, I did not really get into superheroes and comic books as much as some of my peers. As you know by now, I was more of a sci-fi, *Star Trek* nerd, fascinated by the superpowers of science. If I was going to stretch my imagination for fictional characters, I wanted some kind of factual basis that the laws of physics and math provided.

Part of the problem I had with superheroes was the whole secret identity thing. You know, when mild-mannered reporter Clark Kent would dash into the phone booth (remember those?), nearest bathroom or coat closet and emerge with the big red *S* on his chest. Or when bored playboy rich guy Bruce Wayne would disappear from the fancy fund-raiser just before Batman showed up to catch the crooks.

Captain James T. Kirk of the *Starship Enterprise*, however, did not need a mask, cape or utility belt. Whether he was in his Starfleet uniform or not, he was always the same—a charming, reckless, intelligent and courageous leader. Similarly, Captain Kirk's first officer, the renowned Mr. Spock, was always his cool, calm, collected and entirely logical self. There was no hiding who they were unless they were trying to avoid the adversarial Klingons.

Despite being fictional, these characters seemed more consistent and integrated to me. There was no deception about who they were, what their mission was or what their abilities were. Superheroes, on the other hand, fretted over keeping their identities under wraps even from family and loved ones. They felt justified in deceiving those around them and denying their status as heroes when not in costume. While I appreciate their need to remain undercover in order to do their job, I prefer authenticity and transparency in people, whether real or fictional.

I realize that this preference makes me sound like the pastor I am, but fittingly enough, it is just who I am. I know that the tendency we have to hide who we really are goes back to Adam and Eve in the Garden of Eden. They disobeyed God, sewed fig leaves to cover their nakedness and hid. Throughout time and history, human beings have often struggled with living in the tension of who they are versus who they want to be—and how they want to be seen by others.

But as Jesus' encounter with the blind man reminds us, once we experience His presence in our lives, our eyes are opened to the fact that we are no longer who we once were.

We are new creatures in Christ!

The Ultimate Visual Aid

When Jesus and His disciples noticed the man who had been blind since birth, the disciples asked the cause of his blindness. They asked if it was the man's sin or the sin of his parents. But Jesus immediately clarified that neither was at fault:

> "It was not because of his sins or his parents' sins," Jesus answered. "This happened so the power of God could be seen in him. We must quickly carry out the tasks assigned us by the one who sent us. The night is coming, and then no one can work. But while I am here in the world, I am the light of the world."
>
> John 9:3–5 NLT

Keep in mind this combined explanation and exhortation occurred just before Jesus went into action. In the role of teacher, Christ seized this perfectly timed moment to provide the ultimate visual aid to illustrate what He had just told His followers. Rather than being caused by anyone's sin, Jesus indicated the man's blindness served as a revelatory reality to showcase God's power in action.

It is noteworthy that Jesus said nothing directly to the blind man—not until after Christ caked miraculous mud over his eyes did He tell him to go wash in the Pool of Siloam (see verse 7). Curiously enough, the blind man did not object, did not question why this stranger was placing mud over his sightless eyes, did not ask the stranger's identity, did not try to stop the very personal action being perpetrated on him. The blind man's silent response demonstrated faith in God, particularly since we can assume he had just heard what Jesus told His disciples.

Once again, I suspect there are times when we miss out on the messy miracle being performed in our midst because it does not arrive in the manner we expect. Rather than silently receiving the mud that we must endure before we wash our eyes and see anew, we resist the mud altogether. Or we do not understand what and how God is doing what He is doing, so we step back when the Spirit tries to touch us with holy power. We fail to recognize that having faith in God means surrendering the limitations of our human perspective and trusting His omnipotent, omniscient vantage.

We must realize that wanting to get well requires stepping out in faith. Another man with whom Jesus had an encounter also had a physical disability. Instead of not being able to see, however, he did not have the full use of his legs and had not for 38 years (see John 5). Jesus, on His way to Jerusalem for one of the Jewish festivals, saw this man lying near the Sheep Gate of the temple close to the pool known as Bethesda. Rather than introduce Himself or make mud pies, Christ simply asked the man, "Do you want to get well?" (verse 6).

Now such an obvious question may seem unnecessary or even cruel. It might feel as if the question was intended to taunt this lame man. We are told that this pool was well known for its miraculous healing power after the water would bubble up, presumably when stirred supernaturally by an angel. Crowds of people wanting to be healed—including the blind, the lame and the paralyzed—gathered and waited on the colonnade porches to be the first in the water and experience healing (see verse 3). Clearly, if this man was lying there along with so many others in need, he wanted to be well. Otherwise, why bother to be there, right?

WHEN WE RECEIVE OUR MESSY MIRACLE, OUR LIVES WILL NEVER BE THE SAME.

Which brings us back to Jesus' question. Why would He ask something so seemingly superfluous? Aside from what He observed with His eyes in the situation, the Son of God knew the desires of this man's heart. And yet Christ still chose to ask the man deliberately, "Do you want to be well?"

We can safely assume Jesus was not being unkind to this man. We can also recognize that our Lord was not merely making conversation or chatting to be polite. I am convinced Jesus intentionally asked this question because it is a question that we must answer for ourselves when we, too, encounter His miraculous power in the midst of our mess. The answer may seem obvious, but when we receive our messy miracle, our lives will never be the same.

Divine Intervention

Perhaps the lame man heard Jesus' question as an offer to assist him into the pool when the waters bubbled. It is the kind of question you or I might ask an elderly person who is using a cane or walker when we encounter them on a street corner waiting for the crosswalk light to change. Instead of asking, "May I help you cross the street?" we ask in a way that makes the recipient of our offer less beholden: "Would you like to cross the street?" In other words, we take the emphasis off ourselves and place it on the need of this person.

Based on how the lame man answered Jesus' question, such an assumption seems likely. But then what followed was surely not what this man expected to hear:

> "Sir," the invalid replied, "I have no one to help me into the pool when the water is stirred. While I am trying to get in, someone else goes down ahead of me." Then Jesus said to him, "Get up! Pick up your mat and walk." At once the man was cured; he picked up his mat and walked.
>
> John 5:7–9

Basically, this man answered Jesus by explaining that because of his infirmity, he was always too slow to get to the water in time.

The man implied that if he only had someone to help him get to the pool faster, then he would receive the miracle of healing he was there to experience. Perhaps he hoped that this inquisitive stranger would be kind enough to offer some assistance.

Instead, Jesus told the man to get up, pick up the mat he was lying on and walk. The man was healed instantly, and he obeyed as he had been instructed. He needed no one's help to get up and go down to the pool of Bethesda. He needed no assistance to be first in the water. In fact, he did not even need the water! At once the man must have felt the nerves, muscles and bones in the lower half of his body come alive with sensation. He did not hesitate to stand on his own, to pick up his mat or to walk away.

This healing intrigues me. I am intrigued as much because of the way Jesus performed it as I am by the spiritual power He displayed. While He did not make mud or use water from the nearby pool, Jesus still required the lame man's participation through faith. "Do you want to be well?" was not a rhetorical question but a turning point presented to an invalid who falsely believed he was powerless.

Miracles in our messes require our participation. We often passively wait on God and then blame our suffering on what we lack, on other people or on bad timing. But I believe God is waiting for us to stand up, pick up our mat and walk. We assume we are powerless even while knowing we have the living, all-powerful Spirit of God dwelling in us. So we lie around and wish someone could do for us what only we can do for ourselves.

The lame man had been waiting and waiting and waiting—for 38 years—and no one had come through for him. He presumably still harbored hope because, after all, he kept coming to the pool. It seems logical that he blamed his ongoing suffering on his inability. He viewed his healing as being conditional based on variables beyond his control. Getting there with his mat and waiting for the waters to bubble was the best he thought he could do.

But then Jesus intervened and asked if the man wanted to be well.

Christ is asking you the same question, "Do you want to be well?" *Do you want My miracle in the midst of your mess? Do you want My Spirit unleashed in your life? Do you want to open your eyes to the new you?*

Who's Who

No matter what your circumstances may be right now, you have options.

You can remain in a victim mindset like the lame man, or you can embrace the healing power of the Holy Spirit in your life. There is also the option to believe you can control your circumstances by your own power, which is the choice we see made once again by the religious leaders in response to witnessing the miracle strolling by them. You will notice that once the lame man walks, the situation looks remarkably similar to what the blind man experienced after he washed the mud from his eyes:

> The day on which this took place was a Sabbath, and so the Jewish leaders said to the man who had been healed, "It is the Sabbath; the law forbids you to carry your mat." But he replied, "The man who made me well said to me, 'Pick up your mat and walk.'" So they asked him, "Who is this fellow who told you to pick it up and walk?" The man who was healed had no idea who it was, for Jesus had slipped away into the crowd that was there. Later Jesus found him at the temple and said to him, "See, you are well again. Stop sinning or something worse may happen to you." The man went away and told the Jewish leaders that it was Jesus who had made him well.
>
> John 5:9–15

We find that the Jewish religious leaders are at it again—with "it" being ignoring the miracle in front of them and instead focusing on the minutia of the law. Once again, this healing takes place on the Sabbath, a sacred day of rest with strict laws about what one could and could not do. Apparently, the do-not list included carrying your mat around, even if you were taking it home after having been healed miraculously.

When the newly healed, fully ambulatory man told the religious leaders that he was simply complying with the instruction of the person who healed him, they wanted to know the identity of this healer. My suspicion is that they already had a good idea that it was Jesus who had healed this man, but if they could get this witness to identify Him, then they could bring the law down on Him. This seemed to have been their goal time and again.

The man who had been healed apparently did not know his benefactor's name, leaving the Pharisees to fume in their own indignant frustration. But the man's ignorance did not last long. As Jesus did with the blind man that He healed, Jesus came to him and revealed Himself. And yet again, Jesus instructed the man to repent, making clear His power to heal body and soul. Now that he knew the name of his healer, the man informed the Jewish leaders.

Not surprisingly, they began to persecute Jesus (see verse 16). In His defense, Jesus explained, "My Father is always at his work to this very day, and I too am working" (John 5:17). This truth only incensed the religious leaders, however, because now Jesus was not only breaking Sabbath law, but He was referring to God as His Father. Despite elaborating on who He was and why He was there, Jesus became the target of the Jewish religious establishment. They obviously did not want to be well nor were they willing to walk by faith.

They wanted to know Jesus' identity; but even after He revealed Himself to them, they hated Him. They could not control Him, nor, as we know, could they kill Him.

You have the same choice. When confronted with the revelation of Christ in your midst, you can blindfold yourself like the Pharisees, or you can open your eyes and experience the joy of being a forgiven child of God.

The Logic of Loss

When you begin a relationship with the living God, you discover that He loves you too much to allow you to remain in your sin. He loves you too much to allow you to stay in the mud where you are. He loves you too much to let you run from the consequences of past mistakes when He wants to redeem them.

It is not that God is not willing to accept you right where you are—because He absolutely is. But He wants more for you than you can see for yourself at first. Your Creator wants you to thrive and flourish, to grow and blossom in order to bring to life all that He has placed within you. Allow me to remind you, though, of your part in this process: in order for God to complete His miracle in your mess, you have to invite Him into every area of your life. You have to be willing to stand up, grab the mat you have been lying on and start walking. You have to be willing to leave the old you behind.

HE LOVES YOU TOO MUCH TO ALLOW YOU TO STAY IN THE MUD WHERE YOU ARE.

This departure sounds easier to do than it is to complete. Most of us gravitate toward that which is familiar and comfortable. As long as God allows us to stay within our comfort zone, we have no problem remaining faithful and obedient. When the Lord calls us into new territory, though, our trepidation often leads to hesitation. We fear the unknown because our imagination begins working overtime to come up with worst-case scenarios. Rather than trust God and step forward, we often get stuck in place.

We know we cannot go back, and yet our fear prevents us from going forward. Consider the courage that was required for two women to leave the place they knew as home and venture across unknown borders. One of them, Naomi, had lost everything and everyone she loved. She and her husband, Elimelech, had left their hometown of Bethlehem many years prior due to the severe famine and a diminished food supply. They settled in Moab, where they raised two sons, Mahlon and Kilion. After Elimelech died, these sons matured into adulthood and married local women (see Ruth 1:1–3).

Then about ten years later the unthinkable, unimaginable and unbearable happened. Both of Naomi's grown sons died. We are not told how or when or what happened. We do not know whether they died together or separately. We can imagine, however, the grief, anguish, fear and anxiety experienced by their loved ones.

Naomi had lost all her immediate family, her husband and her sons, which in the patriarchal culture of her time meant losing the breadwinners in her family. Hearing that the harvest was plentiful in her homeland, Naomi decided to leave Moab. Her two daughters-in-law, Orpah and Ruth, insisted on going with her. But in a logical rebuttal that would make Mr. Spock proud, Naomi said:

"Why should you go on with me? Can I still give birth to other sons who could grow up to be your husbands? No, my daughters, return to your parents' homes, for I am too old to marry again. And even if it were possible, and I were to get married tonight and bear sons, then what? Would you wait for them to grow up and refuse to marry someone else? No, of course not, my daughters! Things are far more bitter for me than for you, because the LORD himself has raised his fist against me."

Ruth 1:11–13 NLT

From a human perspective, Naomi's argument makes sense. It is the logic of loss. She is too old to marry again and have more sons. And even if by some miracle that did happen, these two younger women would be forced to wait too many years for any sons of Naomi. No, they should stay put, in their own homeland of Moab, and hope for new husbands there.

What is striking about Naomi's argument, though, is her conclusion. "I'm far worse off than either of you because God has it in for me," she basically said. In other words, you two younger women, although also widows like me, have more options, while God has left me with nothing.

Orpah consented to her mother-in-law's logic and stayed in Moab. Ruth, however, pledged her love and loyalty to Naomi and refused to abandon her. Apparently, this response left the older woman speechless, and the two continued on their journey. Despite Ruth's devotion to her, though, Naomi clung to her victim mindset after reaching Bethlehem.

"Don't call me Naomi," she responded. "Instead, call me Mara, for the Almighty has made life very bitter for me. I went away full, but the LORD has brought me home empty. Why call me Naomi when the LORD has caused me to suffer and the Almighty has sent such tragedy upon me?"

Ruth 1:20–21 NLT

Instead of trusting God through her valley of shadows, Naomi became bitter. So bitter that she falsely believed that God had abandoned her.

Bitter or Blessed

When life seems to collapse and leaves us reeling, we often do the same thing Naomi did. We focus our identity on what has happened to us and blame God for allowing such painful circumstances. Naomi went as far as giving herself a name to suit who she felt she had become in the wake of so much loss and pain. We might not admit it to others, but we often do the same.

You might keep your bitterness to yourself, but your identity is not secret to others. Perhaps you are resentful that someone less qualified got the job you deserved. You might be a single parent and blame everything that happens on your divorce and the spouse who is no longer around. Or your parents might receive the brunt of your blame because of the traumatic dysfunction of your home when you were growing up.

Depending on the struggles you are facing, you may have changed your name to *Addict* or *Thief*. You may consider your identity to be *Faker* or *Hypocrite*, or perhaps *Cheater* or *Deceiver*. Your circumstances may leave you identifying as *Always Alone* or *Unforgivable*.

But this default label is not who you really are, of course. The enemy will try to keep whispering it in your ear and bringing up your past losses and mistakes. No matter what he says, though, your past no longer defines you. God promises He will never abandon or forsake you, my friend. He only asks that you continue trusting Him, even when you feel as bitter as Naomi and as blind as the man Jesus encountered near the temple.

This kind of faith requires patience and perseverance. Naomi's story, as you may know, did not end with her remaining a bitter old woman back in Bethlehem. Thanks to Ruth, Naomi took part in the miraculous discovery of who God made her to be. With Naomi's encouragement and counsel, Ruth met and trusted a local man named Boaz. Their relationship led to marriage and to a child, who went on to become the grandfather of King David, the ancestor of Jesus.

> Then the women of the town said to Naomi, "Praise the LORD, who has now provided a redeemer for your family! May this child be famous in Israel. May he restore your youth and care for you in your old age. For he is the son of your daughter-in-law who loves you and has been better to you than seven sons!" Naomi took the baby and cuddled him to her breast. And she cared for him as if he were her own. The neighbor women said, "Now at last Naomi has a son again!" And they named him Obed. He became the father of Jesse and the grandfather of David.
>
> Ruth 4:14–17 NLT

Naomi claimed that her identity was bitter, but God said that it was blessed!

No Laughing Matter

Before her perspective changed, Naomi struggled to leave her old identity as a victim behind her. She realized God had a plan all along, one that she simply had not been able to see previously because her vision had been focused on the horizontal instead of the vertical. As God's plan for her, and for Ruth and Boaz, unfolded, Naomi opened her eyes to the Lord's goodness.

Sometimes when we learn to see spiritually and leave the blindness of our old self behind, we also see more clearly who we are. On several occasions in the Bible, individuals experiencing God received a new name to emphasize the distinction between who they used to be and who they were now in God's eyes. God told Abram, who was almost one hundred years old at the time:

> "This is my covenant with you: I will make you the father of a multitude of nations! What's more, I am changing your name. It will no longer be Abram. Instead, you will be called Abraham, for you will be the father of many nations."
>
> Genesis 17:4–5 NLT

The difference between the names Abram and Abraham is subtle but significant. The name *Abram* means "exalted father"[1] while *Abraham* means "father of many nations" (see Genesis 17:5). As I see it, this shift goes from the general to the specific, revealing the unique, God-given name that reflects who Abraham was created to be.

Addressing someone as *exalted father* might apply to any older man regardless of whether he had children. On the other hand, *father of many nations* indicates that this man is the original patriarch for countless generations around the world. This man not only has children, but he has grandchildren and more great-greats than you can count!

What I love about Abraham's new name is that it immediately brought up a problem: He and his wife—whose name used to be Sarai, but God changed it to Sarah—had no biological children. How could he be the father of many nations if he had no children with his wife? God told Abraham, "Sarah, your wife, will give birth to a son for you. You will name him Isaac, and I will confirm my covenant with him and his descendants as an everlasting covenant" (Genesis 17:19 NLT).

In fact, when Sarah heard this news, she laughed because it seemed so implausibly outrageous. Afraid that her laughter betrayed her lack of confidence that God would give them a son, Sarah denied laughing. But the Lord knew and assured her, "Is anything too hard for the LORD?" (Genesis 18:14 NLT).

Allowing God to produce a miracle in your mess may seem impossible, but nothing is too hard for the Lord our God! *How you see God's power in your life is no laughing matter.* Because as Sarah and Abraham learned, God always follows through on His promises. Sure enough, the couple conceived and had a son named Isaac, which fittingly enough means "laughter." Isaac later had twin sons, Esau and Jacob, and like his grandfather Abraham, Jacob went on to shift from his old identity to a new one given by God—Israel (see Genesis 32:28).

> **ALLOWING GOD TO PRODUCE A MIRACLE IN YOUR MESS MAY SEEM IMPOSSIBLE, BUT NOTHING IS TOO HARD FOR THE LORD OUR GOD!**

Despite the obstacles to their faith, both Abraham and Israel learned to let go of how they saw themselves. They began to instead embrace who God said they were. They stopped looking back and opened their eyes to the divine destiny awaiting them. If we want to experience who God made us to be, then we, too, must complete this same shift in perspective.

The New You

There are two "yous": the old you and the new you.

The old you speaks to the broken you, the fallen you, the sinful you, the fleshly you, the depressed you, the cursed you, the barren you, the victim you and the dead you. The old you likewise reflects the you that survived but never thrived, the you that was touched but was not transformed, the you that saw God's back but not His face, the one who left Egypt but got stuck in the desert. This is the you that grew up with religion but never grew into relationship, the one that got out of hell but never truly brought down heaven.

But the new you knows who you really are. The new you speaks to the saved you, the delivered you, the healed you, the baptized you, the bought you, the blessed you, the forgiven you, the free you, the favored you, the anointed you. The new you is the blood-washed, Christ-redeemed, Bible-based, Spirit-filled, Father-embraced, devil-rebuking, demon-binding, hand-laying and righteousness-pursuing you.

The new you is none other than the chosen you, the prophetic you, the conquering you, the ruling you, the reigning you, the life-changing you, the thriving you and the glorious you. Here is what is true about you: The old you is dead. The old you is buried. The old you will never come back. Right now, I want you to read this out loud: I'm not who I used to be! The old me is dead. The old me is buried. The old me is gone.

In Jesus, through Jesus, with Jesus and because of Jesus, *the new me is alive and well!*

> If the old way, which brings condemnation, was glorious, how much more glorious is the new way, which makes us right with God! In fact, that first glory was not glorious at all compared with the over-whelming glory of the new way.
>
> 2 Corinthians 3:9–10 NLT

Naomi and Ruth, Abraham and Israel are not the only men and women we see in Scripture who experienced both the old and the new. The old Moses died in the desert of disappointment. The new Moses rose on top of the Mount of Transfiguration. The old Peter fell in the water and then denied Jesus three times, but the new Peter came out of an upper room, stood up, started to prophesy and changed the world. The old Saul persecuted those who followed Jesus Christ. The new Paul preached the Gospel of Jesus Christ to anyone and everyone.

Like them, you are no longer who you once were. While the old you looked at the promise, the new you will possess it. While the old you complained, the new you will conquer. While the old you spoke about the glory, the new you will see the glory!

That is why you do not pray like the old you. You do not praise like the old you. You do not talk like the old you. You do not treat others like the old you. It is a new day and a new season with a new song.

God says, "See, I am doing a new thing! Now it springs up; do you not perceive it?" (Isaiah 43:19).

God says, "Therefore, if anyone is in Christ, the new creation has come: The old has gone, the new is here!" (2 Corinthians 5:17).

God says, "Being confident of this, that he who began a good work in you will carry it on to completion until the day of Christ Jesus" (Philippians 1:6). Your new identity in Christ is no secret.

Open your eyes to the power of who God has made you to be!

OPEN YOUR EYES

We often struggle to see ourselves clearly as a new creature in Christ because we continue to focus on our past instead of our future. Like the man born blind who experienced the muddy miracle of Jesus, you must be willing to obey and wash away the impurities that are impeding your vision. Like the lame man healed by Christ near the Pool of Bethesda, you must be willing to get up, grab your mat and step forward. Like the giants of the faith that we find in Scripture—Abraham, Israel, Ruth and Naomi—you must be willing to let go of the old you in order to discover the new you.

Use these questions and the prayer-starter below to help you see clearly as you open your eyes to the reality of who you are in Christ.

1. What are the labels and names that you associate with the old you? How do they still obstruct your vision of who you are in Christ?

2. When have you grown bitter because you failed to see what God was doing in the midst of painful circumstances? How have you seen God's faithfulness even during those times?

3. How have you changed since welcoming Jesus into your life? How does focusing on your new identity in Christ help you experience more of God's power through the Holy Spirit?

Dear Lord, thank You for the new me, the me that You are transforming into the image of Your Son, Jesus. Continue to open my eyes, Father, so that I might focus on where You are leading me, not where I have stumbled in the past. Give me strength to step out of the comfort zone of who I used to be to walk boldly into the glorious future of who I am in Christ. I give You thanks and praise that nothing is too hard for You. Through the power of Your Spirit in me, I know that I am more than a conqueror. In Jesus' name, Amen.

Point of View

Open Your Eyes to Eternity

You cannot embrace what God has for you until you first accept what God did for you.

Once you see by the power of God's Spirit, your entire perspective changes.

I am not one to get starstruck, but I have immense respect for people who excel in their fields.

I was reminded of this recently while I was in Los Angeles for meetings about an opportunity to produce a new film. As an executive producer for the faith-infused films *Breakthrough* and *Flamin' Hot*, I have enjoyed meeting and learning from a wide array of industry professionals.

Not only was I amazed by the couple dozen people gathered in a conference room to discuss project possibilities, but I also gained a greater appreciation for the individuals behind the history of filmmaking by strolling down nearby Hollywood Boulevard. For nearly fifteen blocks, I stargazed along the Hollywood Walk of Fame, looking down at the names of the many familiar celebrities honored.

There were iconic actors from film and television, legendary directors and producers, broadcast radio hosts and recording artists. Each one was honored by a brass star embedded in a square of terrazzo, a composite material of chipped stones that was leveled into the sidewalk. Some were from the early twentieth-century silent films while others showcased Golden Age stars and their visionary directors. Music superstars spanned the decades as well, from jazz and big-band recording artists to pop, soul, R&B and of course, rock and roll.

Each individual had obviously maximized his or her talent and opportunities to contribute his or her own unique artistry to the world. With a little online sleuthing later, I discovered the Walk of Fame currently has more than 2,700 stars with approximately thirty new ones added each year. Apparently, anyone can nominate someone to receive a star to the Walk of Fame Committee, which then garners approval from the Hollywood Chamber of Commerce's Board of Directors and the City of Los Angeles' Board of Public Works Department.[1]

While countless names may be submitted, the Walk of Fame Committee evaluates nominees based on their professional achievement, longevity (they must have been working in their respective genre for five years or more), community contributions and a guarantee that the star recipient, if selected, will attend their dedication ceremony. Posthumous stars are also awarded after five years from the nominee's passing.[2] The Hollywood Walk of Fame keeps criteria stringent in order to ensure the standard of excellence for its members.

The same is true of most any hall of fame. Not every football player ends up enshrined in Canton, Ohio, at the Professional Football Hall of Fame. Not every singer, guitarist, recording artist or band winds up in the Rock and Roll Hall of Fame in Cleveland. Similarly, it takes more than a twang or slide guitar to be inducted into Nashville's Country Music Hall of Fame. And you have to do more than ride a horse to claim a spot in the Cowgirl Hall of Fame in Fort Worth, Texas! No, only the best make it to a hall of fame, the repository recording their accomplishments and preserving the history of their achievements.

But not every hall of fame requires travel and the price of admission. The Bible is filled with members of the faith hall of fame who continue to inspire us today. They remind us to take our eyes off the temporary and focus on eternity.

They inspire us to keep a Spirit-powered point of view.

Believe in Your Benefactor

Throughout our exploration of Jesus' encounter with the man who was blind since birth, we've noted the essential catalyst for experiencing a miracle in our mess is faith. The blind man displayed faith as he silently allowed a stranger to spit, mix mud on the ground and apply this concoction over his eyes. When Jesus told this man to go wash in the Pool of Siloam, he did not ask questions, resist such an unorthodox method or run away. He did not require an explanation, a justification or a guarantee. The man obeyed because he had a faith in God that was bigger than what he could or could not see.

As he followed the familiar route to the Pool of Siloam in darkness, this man must have been quite the sight. Well-known throughout the community as a blind beggar, he walked along wearing a mask of mud over his eyes. He did not go to a nearby well and wash his face. He did not ask someone for water in a basin. This man went where he was instructed by the Maker of miracles—to the Pool of Siloam—and did as he had been told.

The results completed the miracle Jesus set in motion in the man's presence. For the first time in his entire life, this man opened his eyes and saw lights, images, colors and textures. Faces of people who had previously only been recognized as voices came into focus. The blue of the sky, the green of the trees, the colors of the woven fabric worn by women in the marketplace. This man received the gift of sight he had been given unexpectedly, and he recognized the power of God at work even before he learned Jesus' name.

When Jesus asked him if he believed in the Son of Man, the man replied, "Who is he, sir? I want to believe in him." The way Jesus then disclosed His identity appealed to the man's senses. "'You have seen him,' Jesus said, 'and he is speaking to you!'" How ironic that this man who had been blind since birth could now see the benefactor of his blessing along with hearing Jesus' voice. Seeing and hearing was more than enough evidence because the man did not hesitate to affirm, "Yes, Lord, I believe!" (John 9:35–38 NLT).

In light of the miracle this man experienced, he placed his faith in Christ and then worshiped Him. He knew firsthand the person standing before him was God's Son. We might assume faith came easier for him because of the miracle he received, but before we make such an assumption, we might first wonder why we continue to waver in our faith despite the miracles God continues making from our messes. No matter how often God has provided for us in the past, we are still prone to worry about whether and when He will do so for us in the present. Regardless of the miraculous moments in which the Holy Spirit has empowered us to persevere, we continue wondering if we can keep going.

No matter how much we have received, we still struggle to believe in our Benefactor.

Blessed for Believing

It is the same streak of doubt we see in one of Jesus' disciples after the resurrection. Despite the signs, wonders and miracles Thomas had witnessed, despite the personal relationship he had with the Lord, after Jesus was crucified and buried, he wanted proof of His resurrection:

> Now Thomas (also known as Didymus), one of the Twelve, was not with the disciples when Jesus came. So the other disciples told him, "We have seen the Lord!" But he said to them, "Unless I see the nail marks in his hands and put my finger where the nails were, and put my hand into his side, I will not believe." A week later his disciples were in the house again, and Thomas was with them. Though the doors were locked, Jesus came and stood among them and said, "Peace be with you!" Then he said to Thomas, "Put your finger here; see my hands. Reach out your hand and put it into my side. Stop doubting and believe." Thomas said to him, "My Lord and my God!" Then Jesus told him, "Because you have seen me, you have believed; blessed are those who have not seen and yet have believed."
>
> John 20:24–29

Do you hear that? Jesus said we are blessed for believing. The newly sighted man and Thomas and many others who encountered Jesus in person during His time on earth got to experience Him for themselves. They participated firsthand in miracles, in healings and in unimaginable moments of Christ's spiritual power being demonstrated.

There is nothing wrong with wanting evidence as the basis of your faith, but all the evidence in the world is no substitute for trusting God with every area of your life. Clearly, not everyone who met Jesus in person placed their faith in Him as God's Son. Faith transcends physical evidence and relies on our experience of the spiritual. As the apostle Paul explains, "Faith shows the reality of what we hope for; it is the evidence of things we cannot see" (Hebrews 11:1 NLT).

WE ARE BLESSED FOR BELIEVING.

Using that simple, brilliant definition of faith as his starting point, Paul then ushers us into the Faith Hall of Fame and points out exhibits better than any docent or tour guide. "Through their faith, the people in days of old earned a good reputation. By faith we understand that the entire universe was formed at God's command, that what we now see did not come from anything that can be seen" (Hebrews 11:2–3 NLT).

From there, Paul begins with Abel and his pleasing offering to God. He then leads us chronologically through a Who's Who in the Old Testament. Enoch is next, noted for being taken up by God rather than dying because Enoch pleased God. This hall of fame member reminds us that "it is impossible to please God without faith. Anyone who wants to come to him must believe that God exists and that he rewards those who sincerely seek him" (Hebrews 11:6 NLT).

Let's linger for a moment here before continuing our tour. It is impossible to please God without faith. If you want to come to God, then you must believe He exists. You must believe He rewards those who sincerely seek Him.

Do you believe?

A Heavenly Homeland

After Enoch, we go on to Noah (see verse 7) before taking in the enormous faith displayed by Abraham (see verses 8–10) and his wife, Sarah (see verses 11–12). These pillars of faith are all the more remarkable because of what they *did not* see—God's plan completed through the death and resurrection of His Son, Jesus Christ:

> All these people died still believing what God had promised them. They did not receive what was promised, but they saw it all from a distance and welcomed it. They agreed that they were foreigners and nomads here on earth. Obviously people who say such things are looking forward to a country they can call their own. If they had longed for the country they came from, they could have gone back. But they were looking for a better place, a heavenly homeland. That is why God is not ashamed to be called their God, for he has prepared a city for them.
>
> Hebrews 11:13–16 NLT

Notice that these faith practitioners did not consider earthly destinations their home. Instead, they remained faithful as foreigners and nomads on a spiritual journey—not the physical pursuit of comfort, wealth and convenience. If they had focused on these earthly goals, they would have turned away from God and gone down their own path. But they wanted more than what this world can offer. They wanted to be with God in their heavenly homeland.

Moving on from this monumental exhibit, we come to Abraham and Sarah's son, Isaac, the father of Jacob—the God-given namesake known as Israel (see Hebrews 11:20–21). Jacob's son Joseph is then recognized for having faith that God's people would leave Egypt (see verse 22), which leads right into Moses, the leader God chose to confront Pharaoh and guide the Israelites out of slavery, through the Red Sea and into the freedom of the Promised Land (see verses 23–28).

The people of Israel are commended for their faith in following Moses, not turning back when cornered against the Red Sea, and for marching around Jericho for seven days until its walls came crashing down (see verses 29–30). Rahab, known by her profession as a prostitute in Jericho, stands out for trusting the God of foreigners about to conquer her homeland rather than playing it safe (see verse 31).

After summarizing the people of Israel's greatest hits, Paul recognizes the impossibility of showing us all the exhibits of faith heroes: "How much more do I need to say? It would take too long to recount the stories of the faith of Gideon, Barak, Samson, Jephthah, David, Samuel, and all the prophets" (Hebrews 11:32 NLT). So instead of describing more individuals and their faith choices, Paul summarizes the patterns of God-empowerment he sees throughout Hebrew history:

By faith these people overthrew kingdoms, ruled with justice, and received what God had promised them. They shut the mouths of lions, quenched the flames of fire, and escaped death by the edge of the sword. Their weakness was turned to strength. They became strong in battle and put whole armies to flight. Women received their loved ones back again from death.

But others were tortured, refusing to turn from God in order to be set free. They placed their hope in a better life after the resurrection. Some were jeered at, and their backs were cut open with whips. Others were chained in prisons. Some died by stoning, some were sawed in half, and others were killed with the sword. Some went about wearing skins of sheep and goats, destitute and oppressed and mistreated. They were too good for this world, wandering over deserts and mountains, hiding in caves and holes in the ground. All these people earned a good reputation because of their faith, yet none of them received all that God had promised. For God had something better in mind for us, so that they would not reach perfection without us.

Hebrews 11:33–40 NLT

Notice that Paul again emphasizes that these giants of the faith "were too good for this world" because they kept their eyes focused on God and trusted Him to guide their steps. Their faith resulted in their good reputations as people of God. But they also serve as examples of how God chooses to work not through who appears talented, exceptional, gifted or ambitious by earthly standards. God chooses to work through broken people who have a willingness to trust Him.

> GOD CHOOSES TO WORK THROUGH BROKEN PEOPLE WHO HAVE A WILLINGNESS TO TRUST HIM.

God is attracted to impossible circumstances. Show Him a barren womb, a closed door, a shattered dream, a blocked path, a fortified city, a sealed tomb or a man blind from birth and get ready for Him to show up.

Unnamed, But Not Unknown

While we are not told the blind man's name, he belongs in the Faith Hall of Fame alongside those who are listed. In fact, surely there is an entire wing in this faith hall for people who go unnamed but who are not insignificant. We may not know them by their names, but we surely remember them for their faith, for the risks they took, for the courage they displayed or for the way they trusted God.

Our formerly blind man would be there along with the lame man Jesus healed beside the Pool of Bethesda (see John 5:1–16). Surely the woman with the issue of blood also merits our attention for her faith (see Mark 5:25–34). For twelve long years, she suffered with constant bleeding, saw many doctors and lost all her money paying for them. Instead of making her better, the treatments she received made her worse. She had heard about Jesus, however, and as a last resort she thought, "If I can just touch his robe, I will be healed" (Mark 5:28 NLT).

As her fingers grazed the hem of Christ's garment, this woman experienced instantaneous healing throughout her weary body. Jesus knew immediately that someone had tapped into His healing power, but with so many people crowding around Him, it took Him a moment to spot her. When this woman's eyes met those of her Healer, she fell before Him trembling and acknowledged what had just happened. While anyone else might have been upset or angry, Jesus responded with compassion and kindness: "Daughter, your faith has made you well. Go in peace. Your suffering is over" (Mark 5:34 NLT).

Next to this woman in the Faith Hall of Fame's unnamed exhibits we might find the Canaanite woman who persisted with Jesus similarly determined (see Matthew 15:21–28). This woman was a Gentile, someone from a culture considered unclean by the Jews. Her daughter had been possessed by a demon and had suffered terribly from such evil affliction. When she came to Jesus and begged for mercy for her daughter, He ignored her at first. Then the disciples, annoyed by her begging, urged their Master to send her away.

Rather than sending her away, Jesus explained to the woman that His priority was the lost sheep of Israel. Still, her determination did not waver as she knelt before Jesus and cried, "Lord, help me!" When Christ continued explaining His mission to her, the woman's humble appeal to mercy moved Him:

He replied, "It is not right to take the children's bread and toss it to the dogs." "Yes it is, Lord," she said. "Even the dogs eat the crumbs that fall from their master's table." Then Jesus said to her, "Woman, you have great faith! Your request is granted." And her daughter was healed at that moment.

Matthew 15:26–28

Next to these women of faith, we might also find the Samaritan woman at the well (see John 4:1–42) and the woman caught in adultery (see John 8:1–11), whom we considered in previous chapters. We might also see the poor widow praised by Jesus for her sacrificial offering (see Luke 21:1–4) and the boy who gladly gave up his lunch of loaves and fishes so that Jesus could provide food for more than five thousand hungry people (see John 6:1–14). These people put their trust in the Lord and experienced His miracle that was made from the mess in their midst.

Another beneficiary encountered Jesus only briefly during the final moments of both their lives. During the agonizing final hours as Christ suffered on the cross, two other men were also experiencing a similar punishment. As we can see, though, they each had very different responses to the Son of God between them:

One of the criminals hanging beside him scoffed, "So you're the Messiah, are you? Prove it by saving yourself—and us, too, while you're at it!" But the other criminal protested, "Don't you fear God even when you have been sentenced to die? We deserve to die for our crimes, but this man hasn't done anything wrong." Then he said, "Jesus, remember me when you come into your Kingdom." And Jesus replied, "I assure you, today you will be with me in paradise."

Luke 23:39–43 NLT

These individuals might not be as familiar as others whose lives are recounted in greater detail, but their demonstrations of faith stand out just as much. Along with their counterparts named by Paul in Hebrews 11 and many others mentioned in Scripture, they share a common divine denominator. They share a willingness to see beyond what their eyes glimpsed in the physical world around them and a determination to open their eyes to eternity. They could have accepted the limitations imposed by their disabilities, disadvantages and detriments, but they refused. Instead, they chose to place their trust in the living God. In return, they experienced an eternal transformation.

You have a similar choice, my friend. While your circumstances may vary or your limitations may feel more debilitating than those found in the Faith Hall of Fame, I assure you with the truth of God's Word that there is nothing new under the sun (see Ecclesiastes 1:9). You, too, can choose your point of view. Your eyes can remain horizontally focused on today, or the eyes of your heart can vertically align with God's eternal perspective.

Are you looking down or up?

Are you looking sideways or heavenward?

Are you looking around you or beyond you?

The direction of your vision determines your focus.

Negative Space or Positive Faith

What you see spiritually is a matter of perspective just as much as the way that you see physically relies on your vantage point. Photographers and visual artists know that perspective in their work depends in large part on the position of their lenses and its expanse. Dimensionality depends on showing depth and texture, with sharpness of clarity moving from the background to the foreground.

But some images are designed to illustrate the dynamic, subjective tension in how viewers see them. You have probably come across optical illusions and 3-D puzzles that seem to shift between different images right before your eyes, one moment revealing a certain image until your vision adjusts and assimilates another. One moment, you see an ornate vase occupying the forefront of a picture; the next, your vision shifts and glimpses the profiles of two people staring at one another. The shift depends on how you interpret the negative space, the empty space around and between the subjects you choose to focus on.

The way you live out your faith works much the same way.

You can experience your life based on the sensory data collected and collated by your human faculties. Many people do. They rely on their intellect to process and proceed based on what they see, hear, smell, taste and touch. If they cannot see it, hear it or sense it, then they falsely believe it does not exist. Living by this kind of vision largely remains stationary, one-dimensional and fixated on negative space. Without the hope of Christ, without the love of the Father and without the power of the Holy Spirit, there is no messy miracle—there is only a mess.

Or you can shift your sight from negative space to positive faith and experience your life based on your relationship with the holy and almighty, living God through the gift of His Son, Jesus, and the power of His Holy Spirit. You can live as the saints of Scripture, those pioneers of faith, both named and unnamed, who chose to trust God more than their human senses. Like the man born blind who felt the Son of God place mud on his face in order that he might receive the gift of sight, you can experience the unprecedented joy of a messy miracle.

Every human being will inevitably encounter pain, suffering and anguish—physical, emotional and psychological. But whether or not they allow their life's painful events and grievous losses to blind them to the spiritual reality of Christ is their choice. God's Word reminds us, "For our light and momentary troubles are achieving for us an eternal glory that far outweighs them all. So we fix our eyes not on what is seen, but on what is unseen, since what is seen is temporary, but what is unseen is eternal" (2 Corinthians 4:17–18).

So what will you choose to fix your eyes on?

What is seen and temporary?

Or what is unseen and eternal?

Join the Chorus

If you want to live by faith and open your eyes to eternity, then you must recognize who you are in Christ. Following His example, we gaze at others with concern, compassion and kindness. We see beyond momentary problems and focus on eternal solutions. We see through the schemes of the devil and fix our eyes on the Author and Finisher of our faith. We recognize our own sin and receive forgiveness and grace from God.

When you open your eyes to eternity, you realize you are part of a cause much bigger than yourself. Like the members of the Faith Hall of Fame, you know that earth is not your home and that its pleasures are not your goal. When you live by spiritual faith and not by physical sight, you discover that loving, pleasing and serving God is all you desire.

> You are coming to Christ, who is the living cornerstone of God's temple. He was rejected by people, but he was chosen by God for great honor. And you are living stones that God is building into his spiritual temple. What's more, you are his holy priests.
>
> 1 Peter 2:4–5 NLT

You are holy not because of what your eyes see but how your heart sees. You are holy not because of what you do but because of who Christ is. You are holy not because of your actions but because of the Spirit's presence. God is building something in your life that will prompt everyone to give Him the glory because He uses imperfect people to advance His perfect agenda and broken people to heal the world.

YOU ARE HOLY NOT BECAUSE OF WHAT YOU DO BUT BECAUSE OF WHO CHRIST IS.

Through you, God's glory will shine through all you say and do. Your friends will give God the glory. Your family will give Him the glory. Even your enemies will give God the glory. They will have to acknowledge that only God could have done the messy miracles they witness in your life.

Stone by stone, day by day, minute by minute and second by second God is building you up. Joining in the chorus of your faith-filled predecessors, you proclaim:

Whatever you put in front of me, I will deal with it!

If you put a wall in front of me, I will shout it down.

If you put a giant in front of me, I will stone him down.

If you put a mountain in front of me, I will move it out.

If you put a river in front of me, I will cross it.

If you hate me, I will love you.

Curse me and I will bless you.

Kill me and I will rise again.

Break me and I will be healed.

Because I have the power of the living God at work in my life!

Take Your Place

Or perhaps you struggle to share this anthem. Perhaps, like the once-blind man, you want to believe, but you wonder where Jesus is. Perhaps you long to open your eyes to eternity but only see today's urgency. You want to take your place in the Faith Hall of Fame someday, but how?

There are things you built in the past that failed. There are relationships, careers, ministries and dreams you built that fell apart. But then you did not build by faith but by sight.

You built on emotion.
You built with the wrong people in your life.
You built with religion but not relationship.
You built with your plans but not His plans.
You built with fear not faith.
You built with doubt and not destiny.
You built with mud and not miracles.

That is why it fell apart. That is why it came down in pieces. But here is the good news: *not this time!* Listen to what Jesus says:

"Therefore everyone who hears these words of mine and puts them into practice is like a wise man who built his house on the rock. The rain came down, the streams rose, and the winds blew and beat against that house; yet it did not fall, because it had its foundation on the rock."

Matthew 7:24–25

This time you will build on the Rock, Jesus Christ, and it will not, cannot, shall not fail. Right now, you are opening your eyes and seeing God move as never before. Right now, you are opening your eyes and experiencing your messy miracle. Right now, you can do all things through Christ who strengthens you.

If you cannot see it right now, you will soon. So be on the lookout for signs the Spirit is working in you. Keep looking to realize when circumstances do not have an impact on your peace and joy, but your peace and joy have an impact on your circumstances.

When you learn to dance in the desert and sing in the storm.

When what God says about you is more important than what people say about you.

When character is more important than reputation.

When actions speak louder than words.

When you learn that what you cannot shake off, God washes off.

When you believe like Abraham, walk like Enoch, conquer like Joshua, pray like Daniel, touch like Esther, shout like Bartimaeus, climb like Zacchaeus, shine like Stephen and live like Jesus.

When a Christ-centered, Bible-based, Spirit-empowered life is the greatest life of all.

If you are struggling to see clearly, then remember that perception is not reality. It may look as though the enemy is winning. It may look as if that problem has the upper hand. But when all is said and done, what looked like your greatest defeat will actually emerge as your greatest victory.

God's grace is all you need—His power works best in weakness (see 2 Corinthians 12:9). When you are weak, then you are strong in the power of the Spirit. There comes a time when God pushes back everything that came up against you. His Word promises, "The LORD himself will fight for you. Just stay calm" (Exodus 14:14 NLT).

By His grace you are saved. By His wounds you are healed. By His love you are transformed. My friend, your messy miracle has already started. So wash away the mud. Open your eyes. Shift your perspective to the eternal.

And watch what God will do!

OPEN YOUR EYES

As our exploration of messy miracles concludes, use the questions below to facilitate a time of review and reflection. Consider how you saw things before you started reading this book and compare them to how you see things now. As you spend some time in prayer, ask God to continue opening the eyes of your heart to the spiritual realities all around you. Allow the Holy Spirit to guide you so that you walk by faith as you look beyond what your mortal eyes can see. Finally, give God thanks and praise for how you are growing in His Spirit, confident in the good work He is completing in your life.

1. What truth, theme or big idea has God opened your eyes to see through the process of reading this book? How does seeing this strengthen your faith in God and what He is doing in your life?

2. Who are the members of the Bible's Faith Hall of Fame who inspire and encourage you the most? How do their examples help you walk by faith and not by sight?

3. What is the messy miracle you are trusting God to perform in your life? How do you see Him at work despite the mud obscuring your vision?

Dear God, You have opened my eyes to so much as I continue on my journey of faith. As I look back, thank You for allowing me to see the many ways You have sustained me, provided for me, protected me and guided me through the peaks and valleys of my life. May I keep my eyes fixed on Jesus as You help me to see all that You want me to do through the power of Your Spirit. Give me patience, Lord, to trust You and accept Your timing. I give You all thanks and praise for the messy miracle You are working in my life right now. Thank You for all You have taught me and shown me through these pages. In Jesus' name, Amen.

Notes

Chapter 1 Sight Unseen

1. "Infant Vision: Birth to 24 Months of Age," *AOA.org*, 2022, https://www.aoa.org/healthy-eyes/eye-health-for-life/infant-vision?sso=y#:~:text=Eye%2Dhand%20coordination%20begins%20to,or%20other%20person%20near%20them.

Chapter 2 Bless Your Mess

1. Ohio State University, "This Is Your Brain Detecting Patterns," *Science Daily.com*, May 31, 2018, https://www.sciencedaily.com/releases/2018/05/180531114642.htm.

Chapter 4 Holy Spit

1. "What Is DNA," *MedlinePlus.gov*, 2021, https://medlineplus.gov/genetics/understanding/basics/dna/.

2. Robert Matthews, "Who Really Discovered DNA?" *ScienceFocus.com*, 2022, https://www.sciencefocus.com/science/who-really-discovered-dna/.

3. "John 14:16," *StudyLight.org*, 2022, https://www.studylight.org/commentary/john/14-16.html.

Chapter 5 Mud Pies

1. "Agriculture and Rural Life," *ExplorePAHistory.com*, 2019, https://explorepahistory.com/story.php?storyId=1-9-4.

2. You can find info on this farmers' market at https://eastonfarmersmarket.com/.

3. Emma Baldwin, "Mary, Mary Quite Contrary," *PoemAnalysis.com*, 2022, https://poemanalysis.com/nursery-rhyme/mary-mary-quite-contrary/.

Chapter 6 Double Blind

1. Scott Draves, "Double Blind," *Edge.org*, 2017, https://www.edge.org/re sponse-detail/27146.
2. "Subject Bias," *Dictionary.APA.org*, 2022, https://dictionary.apa.org/subject -bias.

Chapter 7 Wash Up

1. Biblical Archaeology Society Staff, "The Siloam Pool: Where Jesus Healed the Blind Man," *BiblicalArchaeology.org*, August 31, 2021, https://www.biblical archaeology.org/daily/biblical-sites-places/biblical-archaeology-sites/the-si loam-pool-where-jesus-healed-the-blind-man/.

Chapter 8 Look Again

1. "Counterfeit," *Etymonline.com*, 2022, https://www.etymonline.com/word /counterfeit.
2. Elizabeth Segran, "'The Volume of the Problem Is Astonishing': Amazon's Battle Against Fakes May Be Too Little, Too Late," *FastCompany.com*, May 17, 2021, https://www.fastcompany.com/90636859/the-volume-of-the-problem-is -astonishing-amazons-battle-against-fakes-may-be-too-little-too-late.
3. Ibid.

Chapter 9 No-Secret Identity

1. "Abram," *BibleStudyTools.com*, 2022, https://www.biblestudytools.com/dic tionaries/eastons-bible-dictionary/abram.html.

Chapter 10 Point of View

1. Hollywood Chamber of Commerce, "2023 Selection," *WalkOfFame.com*, 2022, https://walkoffame.com/nomination-procedure/.
2. Ibid.

Samuel Rodriguez is president of the National Hispanic Christian Leadership Conference (NHCLC), the world's largest Hispanic Christian organization, with more than 42,000 U.S. churches and many additional churches spread throughout the Spanish-speaking diaspora.

Rodriguez stands recognized by CNN, Fox News, Univision and Telemundo as America's most influential Latino/Hispanic faith leader. *Charisma* magazine named him one of the forty leaders who changed the world. The *Wall Street Journal* named him one of the top-twelve Latino leaders, and he was the only faith leader on that list. He has been named among the "Top 100 Christian Leaders in America" (*Newsmax* 2018) and nominated as one of the "100 Most Influential People in the World" (*Time* 2013). Rodriguez is regularly featured on CNN, Fox News, Univision, PBS, *Christianity Today*, the *New York Times*, the *Wall Street Journal* and many others.

Rodriguez was the first Latino to deliver the keynote address at the annual Martin Luther King Jr. Commemorative Service at Ebenezer Baptist Church, and he is a recipient of the Martin Luther King Jr. Leadership Award presented by the Congress of Racial Equality.

Rodriguez advised former American presidents Bush, Obama and Trump, and he frequently consults with Congress regarding advancing immigration and criminal justice reform as well as religious freedom and pro-life initiatives. By the grace of God, the Rev. Samuel Rodriguez is one of the few individuals to have participated in the inauguration ceremonies of two different presidents representing both political parties.

In January 2009, Pastor Sam read from the gospel of Luke for Mr. Obama's inaugural morning service at Saint John's Episcopal Church. On January 20, 2017, at Mr. Trump's inauguration, with more than one billion people watching from around the world, Pastor Sam became the first Latino evangelical to participate in a U.S. presidential inaugural ceremony, reading from Matthew 5 and concluding with "in Jesus' name!" In April 2020, Reverend Rodriguez was appointed to the National Coronavirus Recovery Commission to offer specialized experience and expertise in crisis mitigation and recovery to help national, state and local leaders guide America through the COVID-19 pandemic.

Rodriguez is the executive producer of two films: *Breakthrough*, the GMA Dove Award winner for Inspirational Film of the Year, with an Academy Award nomination for Best Original Song, and *Flamin' Hot*, in partnership with Franklin Entertainment and 20th Century Fox. He is also co-founder of TBN Salsa, an international Christian-based broadcast television network, and he is the author of *You Are Next, Shake Free, Be Light*—a number-one *L.A. Times* bestseller—and *From Survive to Thrive*, a number-one Amazon bestseller.

He earned his master's degree from Lehigh University and has received honorary doctorates from Northwest, William Jessup and Baptist University of the Americas.

Rodriguez serves as the senior pastor of New Season Church, one of America's fastest-growing megachurches and number thirteen on Newsmax's Top 50 megachurches in America, with campuses in Los Angeles and Sacramento, California, where he resides with his wife, Eva, and their three children.

For more information, please visit:

www.PastorSam.com

RevSamuelRodriguez

@pastorsamuelrodriguez

@nhclc